Cybersecurity Law

Cybersecurity Law

Protect Yourself and Your Customers

Shimon Brathwaite

BEP BUSINESS EXPERT PRESS

Cybersecurity Law: Protect Yourself and Your Customers

First published in 2019 by
Business Expert Press, LLC
222 East 46th Street, New York, NY 10017
www.businessexpertpress.com

ISBN-13: 978-1-94897-672-5 (paperback)
ISBN-13: 978-1-94897-673-2 (e-book)

Business Expert Press Business Law and Corporate Risk Management Collection

Collection ISSN: 2333-6722 (print)
Collection ISSN: 2333-6730 (electronic)

Cover and interior design by Exeter Premedia Services Private Ltd., Chennai, India

First edition: 2019

10 9 8 7 6 5 4 3 2 1

Printed in the United States of America.

Abstract

Information security refers to a set of strategies for managing the processes, tools, and policies necessary to prevent, detect, document and counter threats to digital and non-digital information. Infosec responsibilities include establishing a set of business processes that will protect information assets regardless of how the information is formatted or whether it is in transit, being processes or is at rest in storage **"Definition from WhatIs. com (n.d.). Retrieved from** https://searchsecurity.techtarget.com/definition/information-security-infosec**."** With the growth and popularization of the Internet, the Internet of things (IOT) and e-commerce information security has become extremely important in most organizations. The IOT refers to the connection of physical devices such as laptops, home appliances, cars, senors and other electronics to one another through the Internet. This mass connection of devices is constantly collecting information on their usage, location and user behaviors and this information is usually sent to and stored in a database somewhere on the Internet. The result of all of this is that organizations now hold and are responsible for a larger volume of information than ever before. Organizations collect this information because information holds financial value, they can use it to create better products, make targeted marketing campaigns and much more. When holding such valuable digital assets organizations need to ensure that they have an adequate amount of information security for the sake of the company and the customers whose information you are holding. In some cases business partners may demand proof of your company's current information security measures before engaging in electronic commerce with you. In addition to demands made by potential business partners, your company is also subject to federal laws, state/provincial laws and industry specific laws. The penalties for not adhering to these laws include a number of lawsuits by customers that are affected in the event of a data breach and fines by the government or state/province. Cybersecurity law has three main components that I will be discussing:

1. Refers to the legislation that dictates the extent to which organizations must protect their data, in particular personally identifiable information (PII) **"Rouse, M. (n.d.). What is personally identifiable information (PII)."** This refers to any data that could potentially identify

a specific individual. Any information that can be used to distinguish one person from another and can be used to de-anonymizing anonymous data can be considered PII, this includes things such as credit cards, home addresses, phone numbers, and so on.

2. There are laws regarding how a company can collect and use the information that it collects from its customers/clients. This part of cybersecurity law deals more with privacy than it does security itself, this part of legislation deals with making it illegal to do things like eavesdrop on someone's phone calls without the user's consent, making it illegal for companies to sell your information to other companies without making you aware, and so on.

3. There are laws that dictate the authority that law enforcement has when interacting with companies during an investigation. It's important as a company that you know your rights so that you aren't pressured into giving up customer information and breaching their privacy and your clients trusts. This portion of the law will mostly apply to management in larger corporations.

Another important aspect I will be discussing is cybersecurity liability, how to avoid being legally liable in the event of a cybersecurity breach. The number of companies suffering from cyberattacks are increasing every year, combine that with cases of employee misconduct and negligence leading to data leakages and you get an increasing amount of class action lawsuits being filed against corporations. Any data breach where having their data stolen has caused someone harm is a potential lawsuit for a company, I will be discussing ways that companies can reduce the likelihood of being at fault in such a situation. There are also ways that companies can receive financial relief to help them recover after suffering a major data breach that I will go over in later chapters. Data breaches have already affected companies like Yahoo, Sony's Playstation Network, Adobe and Target affected 3 billion, 77 million, 38 million, and 110 million users respectively. With the number of cyberattacks companies face increasing every year this number is likely to only increase and this means the risk of lawsuits to companies whose information is still will continue to increase as well.

Keywords

cybersecurity, information security law, cybersecurity legislation, data privacy laws, cyber law and intellectual property, encryption, encryption laws, data ownership, pipeda, phipa, privacy act, data regulation, personally identifiable information, online privacy protection act, cybersecurity law, cybersecurity lawsuits, cyber liability, legal liability, outsourcing liability, outsourcing data privacy, how to outsource data privacy, cybersecurity specific insurance. cybersecurity insurance, cyber insurance, cybersecurity insurance plan, third- party cyber risk insurance, information security policy, data ownership, data privacy and law enforcement, cybersecurity law in canada, cybersecurity law in the united states, how to automate compliance, patch management, lawsuits, internet law, data breaches, digital assets, digital asset protection

Contents

Disclaimer

The information contained in this book is intended solely to provide general guidance on matters of interest for the personal use of the reader, who accepts full responsibility for its use. The information is provided with the understanding that the author and our publishers are not providing legal services. As such, it should not be used as a substitute for consultation. While we have made every attempt to ensure the information contained in this site has been obtained from reliable sources but we are not responsible for any errors or omissions, or for the results obtained from the use of this information. All information in this book are provided "as is," with no guarantee of completeness, accuracy, timeliness or of the results obtained from the use of this information. Laws and regulations are continually changing, and need to be interpreted based on the situation at hand.

CHAPTER 1

Introduction to Information Security Law

This Will Explain the Current Laws Around Information Security that Businesses Need to Be Aware of

One of the most important responsibilities of a business is to protect the sensitive information of their customers. While conducting business you will gather all sorts of personal information such as credit card numbers, home addresses, phone numbers, bank account information and much more. Not only do you have a moral obligation to properly protect this information but as a business you also have several legal obligations to your customers and if this obligations are not met you can face severe financial repercussions. In this book I will breaking down the current legal risks that management needs to be aware of to avoid being found legally liable if any data breaches do occur. Firstly, I'll give some context on why you need to be concerned about data breaches. In 2015, the total amount of *digital assets stolen* via Cybercrime was estimated to be about $3 trillion USD and is expected to grow $6 trillion USD, which is more than the sale of all major illegal drugs combined. Most people tend to think that most of this money is made by e-transferring money to foreign bank accounts or something of that nature, while a fair amount of that does happen a much larger amount of that $6 trillion is made using information that is stolen "Morgan (January 23, 2018)." "Top five cybersecurity facts, figures and statistics for 2018." When cyber criminals break into a company's network they looking for any information that can be leveraged, things like credit card numbers, phone numbers, usernames and passwords, first and last names, and so on. From there the hackers can use this information in a couple of ways to make a profit:

1. Offload cards: any financial information like credit card numbers or usernames and passwords to bank accounts can be used to directly commit financial fraud and rob your customers of their money.

2. Sell customer information: They can sell this personal information to other people who will use it to commit financial fraud or use their contact information to try to scam the individual by impersonating an entity they trust like a bank for example. A full set of someone's personal information can sell from anywhere between $1 to $450, with the median price being $21.35 "Collins (September 15, 2015)." "Here's what your stolen identity goes for on the Internet's black market."

3. Thirdly, they can hijack that person's account using the username and password they found, and usually because people tend to use similar passwords across accounts they can then go and compromise other accounts that individual has on different platforms. In 2012 dropbox was breached by someone that used login information they obtained from a linkedin data breach that occurred earlier that year.

These are just a few of the potential ways that information can be used once it has been stolen from your company. This is where the legal aspect comes in, if your company is found to be negligent in your handling of your customers personal information and that data is stolen and used in a way that causes harm to the customer, you could be found liable and incur even more costs in settling lawsuits. Due to the increase in cybercrime activity in the last decade, governments have begun to implement more cybersecurity legislation demanding the businesses implement specific types of security practices. In the United States in 2017 alone, 42 states combined to pass more than 240 bills related to cybersecurity "Cybersecurity Legislation 2017 - Legislative News, Studies ... (December/January, 2017)." I'll use two of these as examples of what a company needs to be cautious of:

H.B. 180 enacted in Delware: Amends Chapter 12B of Title 6 to update Delaware's law regarding computer security breaches by doing the following; creates a requirement that any person who conducts business in Delaware and maintains personal information must safeguard that information; updates the definition of breach of security by including the unauthorized access, use, modification, or disclosure of personal information and the information that is included in the definition of personal information.

H.B. 2371 enacted in Illinois: Amends the Data Security on state Computers Act, requires certain state employees to annually undergo training by the Department of Innovation and Technology concerning cybersecurity, allows the department to make the training an online course, requires the training to include detecting phishing scams, preventing spyware infections and identity theft, and preventing and responding to data breaches, allows the department to adopt rules to implement the program.

I chose these two examples because they illustrate two of the key things that a company needs to beware of when it comes to avoiding cybersecurity related lawsuits, which I will go into more depth later on. The first is it is your responsibility to safeguard any information that your company collects. This includes things like making sure your data has some form of encryption, ensuring only the necessary employees have access to certain information, collecting non-essential information from customers, collecting information without making it explicitly clear to your clients, and so on.

The second portion has to do with your employees, about 50 percent of all cybersecurity breaches occur as a result of human error. The human element of our business is just as likely, if not more likely to cause you security issues than any of your computer systems themselves. Therefore, it is very important that you provide your employees with the proper training when it comes to dealing with sensitive information. Some examples would include how to properly dispose of paperwork, how to recognize fake e-mails (phishing campaigns), how to securely use remote access and much more. If a data breach occurs as a result of employee negligence and the employee was not properly trained, the liability for any damages the customer incurs usually falls on the shoulders of the company and that's not a situation you want to be in.

References

https://searchsecurity.techtarget.com/definition/information-security-infosec

https://searchfinancialsecurity.techtarget.com/definition/personally-identifiable-information

https://csoonline.com/article/3153707/security/top-5-cybersecurity-facts-figures-and-statistics.html

https://qz.com/460482/heres-what-your-stolen-identity-goes-for-on-the-internets-black-market/

http://ncsl.org/research/telecommunications-and-information-technology/cybersecurity-legislation-2017.aspx

Collins, K. September 15, 2015. "Here's What Your Stolen Identity Goes for on the Internet's Black Market." Retrieved from https://qz.com/460482/heres-what-your-stolen-identity-goes-for-on-the-internets-black-market/

Cybersecurity Legislation. 2017. "Legislative News, Studies. (December/January, 2017)." Retrieved from http://ncsl.org/research/telecommunications-and-information-technology/cybersecurity-legislation-2017.aspx

Morgan, S. January 23, 2018. "Top 5 Cybersecurity Facts, Figures and Statistics for 2018." Retrieved from https://csoonline.com/article/3153707/security/top-5-cybersecurity-facts-figures-and-statistics.html

Rouse, M. n.d. "What is Personally Identifiable Information (PII)?" *Definition from WhatIs.com.* Retrieved from https://searchfinancialsecurity.techtarget.com/definition/personally-identifiable-information

"What is Information Security (Infosec)?" n.d. *Definition from WhatIs.com.* Retrieved from https://searchsecurity.techtarget.com/definition/information-security-infosec

CHAPTER 2

Cyber Law and Intellectual Property

This Chapter Will Address an Important Aspect of Cyber Law Related to Protecting a Companies IP

Intellectual property refers to a work or invention that are a result of creativity to which a person has rights and you may apply for a patent, copyright, trademark, and so on in order to make that product of creativity your own property "What is Intellectual Property? (n.d.). Retrieved from http://wipo.int/about-ip/en/" For examples are Music, Literature, and Software apps. There are many items that offered over the Internet that are considered Intellectual Property and you need to ensure you have properly registered any of your creations or you may have it stolen by somebody else, simply because they knew how the laws worked and you did not.

Copyright: This is the most common and most important Intellectual Property Law, especially when it comes to the Internet. It covers any original work of authorship such as text for a webpage, a software program, blogs, music, and so on. One of the most common ones that are overlooked on the Internet is getting copyright for you software applications. Remember all software apps are created by someone writing code, and just like any written work no two independent works will look exactly the same, if you are found with an app that has the exact same code as someone else you can be sued and vice versa. Be sure to get copyright on IP that involves computer code.

Patents: This is another important form of IP that is usually used to protect your claim to an invention. When it comes to business on the Internet it is usually used for one of two reasons. Firstly, it is commonly used in conjunction with a copyright to protect a new software by excluding others from making, using, selling or important your invention. Secondly, it is used for new online business methods. There are four main types of patents: a design patent which affects the inventor's concept such as how a product looks and last for 14 years. A utility patent which refers to how a product functions and lasts for 20 years. Software patents (which is considered a type of utility patent), which cover how a computer process works. Lastly, there are plant patents, which are used if you have a business where you work with genetically modified plants, it prevents other companies from creating a new species of plant and lasts for 20 years. It's important to keep in mind the type of patent when you are applying to the USPTO to ensure that you are applying to the right one or you will be denied. The average cost of a design, utility and plant patient are $1,000, $8,500, and $1,000 respectively and that doesn't include insurance, which is an additional $2,500, $12,500, and $2,500 respectively.

Trademark/Service Marks: Popularized by companies like Nike with their signature tick and phrase "just do it" a trademark is a mark that distinguishes you from other companies and it can be a logo, phrase, tune or a symbol. Trademark is used to represent a company's product while a product refers to companies that provide services. The benefit of registering your mark is that once you become establish, other companies will not be able to use a similar mark in order to draw from your customer base. Also, you don't want a situation where you've been using a mark for some time, building your brand and then someone else comes along, trademarks it and now they have sole access to a symbol you worked so hard to build up. When making a trademark or service mark application here are some things you want to consider:

- Is my mark too similar to any other businesses?
- Is my mark provocative or immoral?
- Does my mark include any government symbols or anything that might be included on a national flag?

- Does your mark include anything that is location based that may not be solely applicable to your company?
- Is your mark misleading for your product or service?

The laws regarding if a you need to register your mark and how to go about it vary depending on your country, state, and province. However if you are operating in the US, general it is sufficient to register it online with the United States Patent and Trademark Office (USPTO).

Privacy: Any online business is required to protect their customers privacy in regards to their personal information and online activity when interacting with your website. Depending on where you are, the industry you are in and the type of information you collect the level of protection required will vary. This is discussed in detail in the later chapters.

Trade Secrets: A trade secret is any information about a business or business process that would give another person or business a competitive advantage. It must be something that is not generally known or easily obtainable to the public. Some common examples of this are recipes, designs, ideas, algorithms, and formulas. In the event that a trade secret is stolen you as the holder are entitled to payments of money and getting a court order to prevent the secret from being used. You are required to provide the following if you make a claim:

- That your trade secret meets the definition and qualifies for protection.
- Prove that you took reasonable care to prevent the secret from being revealed to others (such as confidentiality agreements).
- You need to prove that the accused party has obtained the secret using "improper means."

Employment Contracts: Some important aspects you want to include are how employees are to use their company e-mail or any other company digital resources. You also want to make sure that your non-disclosure and non-compete clauses explicitly mention the Internet.

References

http://wipo.int/about-ip/en/
"What is Intellectual Property?" n.d. Retrieved from http://wipo.int/about-ip/
   en/

CHAPTER 3

What Are the Corporate Requirements for Cybersecurity?

This Goes into Detail About What Actions Companies Need to Take to Ensure that They Are in Full Compliance with Information Security Legislation

This chapter will discuss some of the things management needs to ensure is in place to avoid lawsuits from angry customers in the event of a cybersecurity incident. The first piece of legislation your company should be concerned with if you a business operating within Canada (in whole or in part) is an act known as PIPEDA which stands for the Personal Information Protection and Electronic Document Act "Wasser, L. A., Lyons, C., & Koczerginski, M. (2017, October)." This federal legislation to all businesses that are federally regulated and applies to the protection of employee personal information and the protection of personal information during the course of commercial activities. The only time PIPEDA would not apply to business operations in Canada is when the providence has substantially similar legislation, in that case the provincial legislation will be applicable in place of PIPEDA. Currently the only other provinces with legislation that would replace PIPEDA are Alberta *Personal Information Protection Act, SA 2003, c P-6.5.*, British Columbia *Personal Information Protection Act*, SBC 2003, c 63. and Quebec *An Act respecting the Protection of Personal Information in the Private Sector*, CQLR c. P-39.1, which I will all discuss later on. PIPEDA has several security requirements for business, with some of the most important ones highlighted as follows:

1. Businesses are responsible for all personal information under their control and must designate at least one individual to ensure compliance with the principles set out in schedule one of PIPEDA.

2. Personal information must be protected by safeguards appropriate to the sensitivity of the information. This one can be tricky because it's not very specific but I will be discussing in this book the industry standard of security measures used to protect the different types of information companies use and make sure that you can prove if necessary that you did have the proper level of protection. These safeguards must protect against theft/loss as well as unauthorized access, disclosure, copying and use or modification. The types of safeguards used by a business should include: (1) Physical protection like lock cabinets, securing company property. (2) Organizational measures such as security clearances and protocols to be followed on collecting and handling customer information. (3) Technology measures such as the use of passwords and mandatory complexity of passwords and the use of encryption. If your company is holding an client information in a database you need to ensure that it is encrypted so that even if someone is able to steal the information it will be useless to them unless they can decrypt the information, which can take up to several years if you are using just an average or better encryption algorithm. So if you're a management level employee, business owner or someone responsible for the legal aspects of your business you want to make sure that you're data is being protected by an encryption algorithm. In Chapter 4, I will go into more depth on the different types of encryption standards, their pros and cons and how you can go about implementing them.

3. As of June 2015 PIPEDA requires that organizations notify the Office of Privacy Commissioner of Canada (the OPC), affect individuals and organizations or government institutions that can reduce the risk of harm if you believe that a breach of your security safeguards poses a "real risk of significant harm" to the individuals whose

information you are protecting. Companies are also required to keep a record of all breaches and If you are found to knowingly not report a breach you can be fined up to $100,000 CAD.

4. Most jurisdiction in Canada have specific laws when it comes protecting health information that is collected, disclosed by health custodians and the protection of personal information held by government bodies.

5. *Some* provinces have passed torts where customers can bring a claim for breach of their privacy even if they have no proof of actual damages caused.

6. In Canada is it illegal to install a computer program on a person's computer without consent, cause a program to be installed without consent and to cause a computer program to communicate with other electronic devices without consent of the owner and this applies if the installer or the target is in Canada.

7. PIPEDA puts limitations on what data can leave the country and gives restrictions how data can be transferred outside the country.

What Data Must Stay in Canada (G., & Server Cloud Canada (July 13, 2018))

PIPEDA makes all private organizations accountable for protecting information during transit and outsourcing, while generally it is legal for information to cross Canadian borders the Canadian business remains liable for any problems with that information. Federal government institutions are subject to the country's *Privacy Act*, which outlines how personal information is stored and collected. If you work for a federal government, you will be held to a higher standard when it comes to information security. There is currently a proposal that would prohibit classified data from leaving the country, period. In Alberta and Quebec, the transfer of public sector personal data outside of the country is restricted and in some cases it's prohibited outside of the province. British Columbia and Nova Scotia prohibit government institutions, Crown agents and their service providers from moving any personal data outside of Canada, with very few exceptions. If you are a business that collects health-related information operating out of Ontario, you can't disclose any of that information without that individual's expressed consent in *PHIPA*, the Personal Health Information Protection Act. If you want to move that health data outside of the province, your company must adhere to PHIPA. Depending on where your company is located in Canada and what type of business you operate, you might be unable to transfer data outside your province or the country or you may only be able to transfer it with certain security measures in place.

Rules that Affect Data Leaving Canada

PIPEDA dictates that companies are responsible for the information they've collected even when you transfer it to a third party. PIPEDA requires that you use "contractual or other means to provide a comparable level of protection while the information is being processed by a third party." Here is a breakdown of what this regulation means:

- **Transfer:** When information is transferred for processing, it must only be used for the original purpose of collection (for instance, marketing).
- **Comparable Level of Protection:** The third party processor must provide an equivalent level of protection the data would have received if it remained with the Canadian company.
- **Transparency:** The organization must be transparent about their practices handling personal information. Organizations must tell customers that their data is sent elsewhere for processing, and state that personal information sent to another jurisdiction may still be accessed by Canadian law enforcement, courts, or national security personnel.

Rules Around Data Storage and Transfers

As I mentioned previously even after transferring personal information outside of your jurisdiction, your company remains accountable for the information even after a third party takes possession of it and starts processing it. Your primary means for protecting yourself from liability once you've transferred information to a third party is a contract where you get the third party to agree to properly protect and handle the information that they are taking into their possession. You also want to take time to question any third-party provider your considering on their data security practices and make sure they have a level of security that is required by provincial and federal data storage and privacy laws. Another responsibility you have is informing your customers about how their data will be handled, this includes informing them that you are sending the information to another jurisdiction. Keep in mind that one data is transferred outside of Canada it becomes subject to the laws of the country where the data is stored, so you need to be mindful of that before agreeing to transfer the data and do a risk assessment to make sure you will not be violated any of these new laws that you're operating under. If possible it's much better to use local cloud service providers because you only have to adhere to Canadian and provincial privacy laws and Canadian providers have the best knowledge of the country's privacy laws, so they're in the best position to securely store data.

In addition to these laws that affect all businesses that do business in Canada, there are also sector specific laws that affect you depending on what your business does. The first I will discuss its effect financial institutions:

The Office of the Superintendent of Financial Institutions (OSFI) regulates all Federal Regulated Financial Institutions (FRFI) which includes banks, most insurance companies, and federal pension plans released a cybersecurity *self-assessment* guide in 2013 for all FRFI to assess their preparation in case of cybersecurity breach and to assist in implementing useful cybersecurity practices. The template is comprised of six categories organization and resources; cyber risk and control assessment; situational awareness; threat and vulnerability risk management; cybersecurity incident management; and cybersecurity governance. It's important to note that while this is a useful template, the OSFI "expects FRFI Senior Management to review cyber risk management policies and practices to ensure that they remain appropriate and effective in light of changing circumstances and risks." Other regulators in Canada that you need to be aware of:

- The Investment Industry Regulatory Organization released a Cybersecurity Best Practices Guide and a Cyber Incident Management Planning Guide in December 2015;
- The Mutual Fund Dealers Association of Canada released a Bulletin on Cybersecurity in May 2016.

The third item you want to have is cybersecurity specific insurance coverage. Due to cybercrime being a relatively new risk to businesses there is a good chance your standard insurance plan will not cover you in the event of a data breach, therefore you want to speak to your insurance provider and make certain that your coverage plan will cover you in the event of a cybersecurity incident. In the event that they do not provide coverage for that, I would need to look into getting specific cybersecurity coverage. In Chapter 6, I go into detail on what cybersecurity insurance coverages are out there, highlight what you need them to cover, give cost analysis and much more.

Lastly, two important privacy related torts that your company needs to be aware of when collecting information from your customers. In 2012, the Ontario Court of Appeal recognized the tort of " intrusion upon seclusion." "One who intentionally [or recklessly] intrudes, physically or otherwise, upon the seclusion of another or his [or her] private affairs or concerns, is subject to liability to the other for invasion of his privacy, if the invasion would be highly offensive to a reasonable person." This tort makes companies liable for collecting personal information without making it explicitly clear to the individual and first getting permission, otherwise it is seen as an invasion of privacy and a lawsuit can be filled.

The second tort your company needs to be aware of was introduced in February 2016 *Jane Doe 464533 v ND:* One who gives publicity to a matter concerning the private life of another is subject to liability to the other for invasion of the other's privacy, if the matter publicized or the act of the publication (a) would be highly offensive to a reasonable person, and (b) is not of legitimate concern to the public. This law's main purpose is to hold people accountable for cyberbullying but it can affect companies if your employees are not careful about releasing information only to those that absolutely need it and only with the consent of the owner of the information.

Rules if Your Business Operates Within the United States

The United States doesn't have a single comprehensive federal law for regulating the collection and use of personal information, the laws that govern business activities are a mix of various state and federal legislation. In addition to these they are guidelines develop by government agencies and industry specific standards that aren't necessarily force of the law but make up what are considered best practices, which are standards that companies are expected to meet. These guidelines can be used by enforcement agencies and regulators in evaluating your business in the event of a data breach. Here are some of the most important legislation to be aware of "(Jolly, L. 2017, July 1)": *Please note* for simplicity the format used was based off of the original content but content of the heading themselves are my own original words.*

The Federal Trade Commission Act (FTC Act): Is a federal consumer protection law that protects against unfair or deceptive practices related to privacy and data security policies that don't protect consumer's personal information.

To Whom Does It Apply?

The FTC act applies to most companies doing business in the US with the exception of certain transportation, telecommunications and financial companies because they are primarily regulated by other national agencies.

What Data Is Regulated?

The FTC act doesn't regulate a specific type of information, it prohibits unfair and deceptive practices put consumer personal information at risk.

What Acts Are Regulated?

The FTC has been used to charge companies that:

- Failed to adequately protect consumer personal data, leaving it open to cyberattacks.

- Changed their consumer privacy policies without providing reasonable notice to consumers.
- Failed to adhere to their posted privacy policies.

Jurisdictional Scope

It applies to companies and individuals who are doing business in the United States.

Exemptions

You can be exempt from the privacy rules and guidelines of the FTC for law enforcement purposes (provided they have a court order/warrant).

Notification Requirements

The FTC doesn't have any requirements, but it suggests that website operators disclose their data collection practices related to behavioral advertising, provide consumers with an option to opt out of these practices and properly notify consumers that they can opt out of these practices.

Main Obligations on Data Collectors

- Ensure that you comply with your privacy policies.
- When you retroactively change a privacy policy, you must give data subjects the opportunity to opt out of a new privacy practice.

Violating the FTC has resulted in lawsuits of up to $100 million, which occurred in a penalty against LifeLock in 2010 for failing to secure customer's personal data.

The FTC suggest that website operators gets express consent (can be online) for sensitive data, which includes:

- Financial data
- Data about children

- Health *Is consent of data subjects required before processing?*
  Information
- Precise geographic location
- Social security numbers

You also need express consent to use consumer data in ways different than outlined in your privacy policy that was in effect when the data was collected. If you website is directed at children or you knowingly collect the personal information of children you are required to get verifiable parental consent before sharing that personal information. The Children's Online Privacy Protection Act, requires that parents be able to view information collected about a child and to delete or correct that information.

Security Requirements

FTC Behavioral Advertising principles that website operates should provide reasonable security for the data that they collect and should retain data only as long as it is necessary to fulfill a business or law enforcement need. While it doesn't specify that constitutes a "reasonable" level of security, it states that consumer data protection should be based upon:

- Sensitivity of the data
- Nature of the company's business operations
- Type of risk your company faces
- Reasonable protections available to a company

Processing by Third Parties

The FTC has several rules such as the Safeguards Rule, the Affiliate Sharing RUle and Affiliate Marketing Rule, which limit the sharing and use of financial information and credit report information with affiliates.

On what conditions can cookies or equivalent be stored on a user's devices:

- You should disclose your data collection practices
- Obtain consent before collecting sensitive information

- Disclose that customers can opt out and provide a mechanism to do so

Enforcement and Sanctions

The FTC is the primary US enforcer of national privacy laws, including the FTC act and penalties for breaking this act can be up to US$16,000 for each offence. In 2006, a data broker agreed to pay US$15 million to settle charges by the FTC for inadequate protection of data. Criminal penalties include imprisonment for up to 10 years. Settling with government agencies can also include reporting requirements such as agreeing to audits and being monitored by third-parties. There have been cases where the audit of a guilty party's data security system lasted for 20 years.

The Financial Services Modernization Act/Gramm-Leach-Bile Act (GLB): This act regulates the collection, use and disclosure of financial information. It affects all businesses that provide financial services and products such as banks, securities firms and insurance companies. It limits the disclosure of non-public personal information and in some situations require that the company provide notice of their privacy practices and give their customers the option of opting out of having their information shared.

To Whom Does It Apply?

It applies to financial institutions, which are defined by the FTC as businesses significantly engaged in financial activities. It also applies to third parties that are not financial institutions but receive personal information from financial institutions.

What Data Is Regulated?

Non-public personal information collected by a financial institution that is provided by, results from or otherwise obtained in connection with consumers or customers who obtain financial products or services primarily for personal, family or household purposes from a financial institution. Non-public information applies to information that is capable of personally identifying a consumer or customer and is not publicly

available. For the purposes of the GLB act a consumer is defined as someone who has obtained a financial product or service but doesn't have an
going relationship, while a customer refers to a person who has an ongoing relationship with the institution.

What Acts Are Regulated?

The GLB act regulates the collection, use, sharing and disclosure of
non-public financial information. Companies are required to implement
a security program to protect non-public personal information and there
are requirements to obtain consent before collecting information and providing opportunities to opt-out of non-essential information disclosures.
Companies are also require to give written notice of privacy procedures.
The requirements of obtaining consent, giving written notice of privacy
procedures and providing opt-out opportunities vary depending on
whether its a consumer or a customer.

Jurisdictional Scope

It applies to financial institutions, affiliated and non-affiliated third parties that receive the nonpublic personal information. It also applies to
any person who obtain or attempt to obtain, or cause or attempt to cause
disclosure of that non-public personal information.

Exemptions

A company can disclose a consumer's non-public personal information
with an affiliated entity, as long as you provide notice. You do not need to
obtain consent for the disclosure. An affiliated entity is any company that
controls, or is controlled by or is under common control with another
company, they can be non-financial institutions.

A financial institution can disclose a consumer's non-public information with a non-affiliated entity without providing the right to opt out if:

- The disclosure is to a third party that uses information to
  perform services for the financial institution.
- The financial institution provides notice of this practice.

- The financial institution and the third party enter into
  a contract that requires the third party to maintain the
  confidentiality of the information and use the information
  only as intended.

A financial institution can also disclose non-public personal information for compliance purposes and law enforcement purposes.

Notification Requirements

Financial institutions are required to provide notice of its privacy practices.

Main Obligations on Data Collectors

You must notify your customers about your information-sharing practices and tell consumers of their right to opt out if they don't want their information shared with non-affiliated third parties. The GLB also has a safeguards rule that requires that you develop a written information security plan that outlines your program to protect customer records and information. You security plan should include:

- Data encryption
- Authentication mechanisms
- Background checks
- Frequent monitoring and testing of information security
  protocols and systems
- Implementing an identity theft prevention program in
  connection with covered **accounts**
- Implementing response program that requires the financial
  institution to notify the regulator when there has been unau-
  thorized access to sensitive customer information.
- Contractually requiring its service provider to ensure that they
  are meeting the objectives of the security program.

Is Consent of Data Subjects Required Before Processing?

You are required at the time of establishing the customer relationship and at least annually after that, to notify customers and consumers of the institution's privacy policy and practices and allow the individual to opt-out of certain disclosures of the individual's non-public personal information.

Security Requirements

As part of its plan, each company must:

- Designate one or more employees to co-ordinate its information security program.
- Identify and assess the risks to customer information in each relevant area of the company's operation, and evaluate the effectiveness of the current safeguards for controlling these risks.
- Design and implement a safeguards program, and regularly monitor and test it.
- Select service providers that can maintain appropriate safeguards, ensure contracts require them to maintain safeguards, and oversee their handling of customer information.
- Evaluate and adjust the program in light of relevant circumstances, including changes in the firm's business or operations, or the results of security testing and monitoring.

The requirements are designed to be flexible, according the FTC companies should implement safeguards appropriate to their own circumstances. You are required to develop a written program that identifies and detects the relevant warning signs (red flags) of identity theft.

Sanctions for Non-compliance

Enforcement action by the FTC can include penalties of up to US$16,000 per offence. Individuals who obtain, attempt to obtain, cause to be disclosed or attempt to cause to be disclosed customer information of a financial institution relating to another person through fraudulent means can face fines and up to five years in prison. Also, If your violation is committed while violating another US law or as part of a pattern of illegal activity involving more than US$100,000 you can face up to 10 years in prison and fines of up to US$500,000 for an individual and US$1 million for a company.

The Health Insurance Portability and Accountability Act (HIPAA): This act regulates medical information.

To Whom Does It Apply?

It applies to health care provider, data processors, pharmacies and any other entities that come into contact with medical information. It also applies to business associates, which is a person or entity that performs certain functions or activities that involve the use or disclosure of personal health information (PHI) on behalf of, or provides services to, a covered entity. Some common examples of this are data analysis and processing, quality assurance and billing.

What Data Is Regulated?

HIPAA regulations PHI, which is individually identifiable health and medical information that is maintained or transmitted by a covered entity or its business associate.

What Acts Are Regulated?

HIPAA regulates the use and disclosure of PHI and the collection, use, maintenance or transmission of electronic PHI. HIPAA also requires that you make customers aware of your privacy practices.

Jurisdictional Scope

HIPAA covers all entities defined in the (to whom does it apply) section, over which the US Government has enforcement authority, additionally business associates of covered entities may have contractual obligations to protect PHI, even those operating outside of US jurisdiction.

Exemptions

HIPAA does not apply to health information that is not personally identifiable.

Notification Requirements

HIPAA requires all entities to provide notice to data owners of your privacy practices and of the data owner's rights under HIPAA. You are also required to notify individuals when their unsecured personal health information has been breached.

Main Obligations on Data Collectors

- You must use, request and disclose the minimum amount of PHI necessary to complete a transaction.
- You should implement data security procedures, protocols and policies at administrative, technical, physical and organizational levels to protect customer information.

Is Consent of Data Subjects Required Before Processing?

HIPAA requires covered entities to obtain consent in written form from all data subjects before disclosing data, with few exceptions such as providing emergency medical treatment. Consent consists of acquiring the signature of the data subject and the date and should be in writing. The *HIPAA Privacy Rule* contains specific statements that must be included in the consent of data subjects. The notice **must** contain the statement: "THIS NOTICE DESCRIBES HOW MEDICAL INFORMATION ABOUT YOU MAY BE USED AND DISCLOSED AND HOW YOU CAN GET ACCESS TO THIS INFORMATION. PLEASE REVIEW IT CAREFULLY." The notice then needs to include:

- The uses and disclosures of PHI that you intend to make
- How a person can access their information
- How to complain about a HIPAA violation
- An effective date

Special Rules

There are specific rules that regulate the disclosure of psychotherapy notes, which means notes made by a health care provider, who is a mental

health professional documenting or analyzing the contents of a con-
versation during a private counseling session or a group, join or family
counseling session, which are separated from the rest of the individual's
medical record. Generally you must obtain written authorization from
the patient before disclosing psychotherapy notes, even for the purposes
of treatment.

Rights of the Data Subject

Under HIPAA, the Data Subject has the right to request access to their
information, make corrections to their own PHI and can request an
account the manner in which his PHI has been used and disclosed.

Security Requirements

The HIPAA requires covered entities to:

- Use and disclose the minimum amount of PHI necessary to
  complete a transaction.
- Implement data security procedures and policies to
  protect data.
- Comply with certain standards established for electronic
  transactions.

There is a separate HIPAA guide for the Remote Use of and Access to
Electronic Protected Health Information which outlines the risks for stor-
ing, accessing and transferring of medial data on laptops, wireless devices,
home computers, flash drives, e-mail and public workstations.

Third Party Processing Requirements

HIPAA allows for regulated entities to disclose PHI to business associates
if you enter into an agreement that your requires your associates to use the
information for the solely the purposes that you have engaged in business
with them for, to safeguard your customers information from any misuse
and to ensure that the business associate complies with any applicable

rules under the HIPAA privacy laws. Once you become aware of a material breach or violation by a business associate, you must take reasonable steps to cure the breach and if you are unsuccessful you should terminate the arrangement. If termination of your agreement is not feasible, you are required to report the problem to the Department of Health and Human Services Office for Civil Rights. The Department of Health and Human Services have sample business associate agreements that you can use for guidance but they are not required to be used. Also, HIPAA does not require that a national regulator approve a data transfer agreement, but a regulator may have audit powers to ensure compliance with HIPAA rules.

National Regulator for HIPAA

HIPAA is enforced by the Office of Civil Rights within the Department of Health and Human Services. They have the power to initiate an investigation into a covered entities information handling practices to determine whether you are complying with the HIPAA privacy rule and allows individuals to file complaints about privacy violations.

HIPAA Sanctions

HIPAA authorizes civil penalties from US$100 to US$1.5 million depending on the following factors:

- Did the operator know the act was a violation
- How quickly was the violation corrected
- Was the operator willfully negligent

Criminal penalties can be up to US$250,000 and/or up to 10 years in jail if the offence was committed under false pretenses or with intent to sell the data for financial gain. Additionally some state and federal laws allow individuals to sue in court for privacy violations. One notable incident was Target in 2013 where the payment card information of over 40 million consumers and the personal information of another 70 million consumers was disclosed and it resulted in the payment of US$18.5 million on May 23, 2017.

The HIPAA Omnibus Rule

This rule requires covered entities to give notice of any breach of protected health information. All covered entities must provide notice of acquisition, access, use or disclosure of PHI in any manner not permitted under the HIPAA privacy rule. The only exception is if the entity or business associate can demonstrate that there is a law probability that the PHI has been compromised.

The Fair Credit Reporting Act

This act is an amendment of the Fair Credit Report act which applies to consumer reporting agencies, people who use consumer reports and people who provide consumer-reporting information. Consumer reports are defined as any communication issued by a consumer reporting agency that is related to creditworthiness, credit history, credit capacity, character and general reputation which is used in evaluating a consumer's eligibility for credit or insurance.

The Controlling the Assault of Non-solicited Pornography and Marketing Act and the Telephone Consumer Protection Act

Regulate the collection and use of e-mail addresses and telephone numbers.

The Electronic Communications Privacy Act and the Computer Fraud and Abuse Act

It regulates the interception of electronic communications and computer tampering. This act heavily affects Internet Service providers, advertising companies and law enforcement agencies.

California Security Breach Notification Law

This law applies to any entity that conducts business in California or owns or licenses data from California, which includes personal information. It requires that in the event of a security breach of personal information, any resident of California whose unencrypted personal information was or is reasonably believed to have been acquired by an unauthorized person, must be notified. Also for any business or person that handles personal information on behalf of your business that you do not own you must notify the owner or licensee of any security breach that has led to a loss of information, immediately following the discovery if you reasonably believe that information was acquired by an unauthorized person. If your business is found to be the source of the breach, you will be required to provide appropriate theft prevention and mitigation services at no cost to any affected person for no less than 12 months. In the event of a security breach, notice should be provided to all individuals in one of the following ways:

- Written notice
- Electronic notice (consistent with national laws about electronic signatures)
- Substitute notice (this can only be done if the company demonstrates that the cost of providing a notice in a written or electronic form would exceed US$250,000, the affected amount of people is greater than 500,000 or the company doesn't have the necessary contact information to use either of the other two notice types).

A substitute notice must include:

- E-mail notice when the company has an e-mail address for the affected people.
- Posting a notice on the regulating agency's website page, if the agency maintains one
- Notifying major state-wide media

You can replace these procedures if your company maintains its own notification procedures via an information security policy for personal information that is consistent with legal timing requirements. You will be considered in compliance if you notify your customers in accordance with the policies you set out in the event of a breach of system security. You must submit a copy of the notification you send to affect customers to the California Attorney General. Since this law is triggered by the disclosure of unencrypted information, it's recommended that you keep all of companies personal information encrypted. If encrypted information is stolen during a data breach it will not require a breach notification because that information cannot be accessed by an unauthorized person without them using extreme measures.

The California Online Privacy Protection Act

This applies to anyone who is operating a commercial website, providing a service online or through a mobile app that uses personally identifiable information collected from their customers. This act requires that commercial websites to post their privacy policies on the website itself, describing in detail its information handling procedures. It also requires that online services and mobile apps that are directed to minors or are aware that a minor is using their services to permit a minor to remove or request the removal of certain online information, disclose how minors can remove or request removal of content and prohibits operators from advertising products not legally available to minors such as alcohol, firearms, tobacco, tattoos, and lottery tickets. During the time of data collection, your Data Privacy Policy must:

- Identify the categories of personally identifiable information that you will collect through the website or online service and the categories of third-party entities that the operator can share that personally identifiable information.
- You must explain how a customer can view their personal information that has been collected for your website and how to make changes to that information if you allow it.
- Explain how you notify consumers of changes to your privacy policy.
- State the effective date of the privacy policy.

Security Requirements

The Ponemon Institute calculated that in 2016 the average cost of a security breach to a company was US$4 million up from US$3.79 million in 2015. Breach prevention and notification is an increasingly costly proposition, with a 12 percent increase in per capita cost just since 2013. In addition to civil and criminal sanctions, security breaches can have far reaching consequences for companies in terms of loss of customer confidence and trust, customer churn, and loss of revenue, market share, brand and shareholder value.

CHAPTER 4

What Are the Financial and Reputational Implications of Information Security Legislation

What Types of Lawsuits Can Be Brought Against a Company that Doesn't Comply with the Current Information Security Laws and How Costly Are They?

If your company is found in a breach of any of the legislation I outlined in Chapter 2 you will be at risk of a potential lawsuit. This chapter I'm going to discuss the different types of lawsuits that your company would be facing and what the financial implications this would mean for your company. In Canada, class action lawsuits tend to fall into three categories: (1) Employee errors (2) Employee misconduct, and (3) data breaches.

Employee Errors: This is a situation where an employee does something unintentionally that results in a breach of privacy of an individual. For example an employee loses a unprotected flash drive that contains the information of customers.

Employee Misconduct: This is a situation where an employee intentionally accesses information that are not authorized to see. It's important to note that just because someone is an employee of a company, doesn't mean they should have access to all of the information the company possesses. To be safe employees should only be given access to information that is essential for them to do their job and nothing more, in information security this is covered under the principle of "least privilege."

Data Breaches: This lawsuits covered situations where information is leaked due to malicious activity by an external party. This would be situations where a hacker breaks into a computer network a steals usernames and passwords, credit card information, and so on. In order to reduce the likelihood of being found liable for these breaches it's very important you meet industry standard with your security measures. These lawsuits tend to have the largest financial burden on a company, for example, $760 million USD with Ashley Madison and $550 million to Equifax. Plaintiffs tend to agree things such as breach of contract, breach of consumer protection legislation, negligence, intrusion upon seclusion, breach of privacy and publicity given to private life.

Cybersecurity Laws in the United States

Federal Laws

1996 Health Insurance Portability and Accountability Act (HIPAA): This is US federal law meant to protect health care patients privacy. It only affects certain members of the health industry such as health care providers, health insurers, and health exchange organizations. HIPAA covers all personally identifiable information that is created or received by the organizations. In addition to HIPAA, health information is also governed by state laws.

1999 Gramm-Leach-Bliley Act: This act requires financial institutions, which is defined as companies that offer consumer financial products or services such as loans, financial/investment advice or insurance to explain their information sharing practices to customers and to safeguard the customers data. Gramm-Leach-Bliley Act (n.d.).

2002 Homeland Security Act, which included the Federal Information Security Management Act (FISMA): FISMA is a framework that gives guidelines on how to protect government information, assets and operations against natural and manmade threats. It requires program officials and the head of each agency to conduct annual reviews of information security programs with the intent of keeping risks at or below acceptable levels.

The National Institute of Standards and Technology (NIST) outlines nine steps toward compliance with FISMA:

1. Categorize the information to be protected.
2. Select minimum baseline controls.
3. Refine controls using a risk assessment procedure.
4. Document the controls in the system security plan.
5. Implement security controls in appropriate information systems.
6. Assess the effectiveness of the security controls once they have been implemented.
7. Determine agency-level risk to the mission or business case.
8. Authorize the information system for processing.
9. Monitor the security controls on a continuous basis.

These three laws together mandate that Healthcare Organizations, Financial Institutions, and Federal Agencies must protect their systems and information with a "reasonable" level of security.

Federal Exchange Data Breach Notification Act of 2015: This *bill* requires a health insurance exchange to notify each individual whose personal information is known to have been acquired or accessed as a result of a breach of security of any system maintained by the exchange as soon as possible but not later than 60 days after discovery of the breach.

State Laws

California implemented a law in 2003 called the Notice of Security Breach act that required any company that maintains personal information of California citizens to notify them in the event of a breach. Since then several other states have implemented similar laws, so if you are conducting business in the United States be aware that in the event of cyber-security incident, you are expected to notify those that have been affected.

The New York State Department of Financial Services (DFS) passed the New York Cyber Security Regulation on March 1st 2017, this requires that all affected companies must submit a yearly Certification of Compliance with the New York State Department of Financial Services Cybersecurity Regulations starting February 15, 2018.

What Are the Technology Requirements You Need to Reduce the Risk of Legal Liability?

Here are some the best practices that your company can implement to make sure that you meet the standard of "reasonable information security," this list consists of 20 controls defined by the Center for *Internet Security's Critical Security Controls (CIS Controls*™ *(n.d.)*. Retrieved from https://cisecurity.org/controls/) which the California Attorney General Otto and Kennedy (2016). "Reasonable Security" Becomes Reasonably Clear to the California Attorney General stated represented "the minimum level of information security":

1. Inventory of Authorized and Unauthorized Devices
2. Inventory of Authorized and Unauthorized Software
3. Security Configurations for Hardware and Software on Mobile Devices, Laptops, Workstations, and Servers
4. Continuous Vulnerability Assessment and Remediation
5. Controlled Use of Administrative Privileges
6. Maintenance, Monitoring, and Analysis of Audit Logs
7. Email and Web Browsing Protection
8. *Malware Defenses*
9. Limitation and Control of Network Ports, Protocols, and Services
10. *Data Recovery Capability*
11. Secure Configurations for Network Devices such as Firewalls, Routers, and Switches
12. Boundary Defense
13. Data Protection
14. Controlled Access Based on the Need to Know
15. Wireless Access Control
16. Account Monitoring and Control

17. Security Skills Assessment and Appropriate Training to Fill Gaps
18. *Application Software Security*
19. Incident Response and Management
20. Penetration Tests and Red Team Exercises

Additional Recommendations Otto and Kennedy (2016).

In addition to these the California Attorney General also stated that usernames and passwords alone were not sufficient to protect a user's personal information. It was recommended that organizations make multi-factor authentication available for consumer-facing online accounts. Multi-factor authentication means that in addition to requiring users to provide something that they know (like a username or password) they must also provide something they have (like a onetime code that is generated and sent via text after the username and password are provided) or something they are (like a fingerprint or retina scan). By doing so it becomes significantly harder for a hacker to compromise the account. Some popular websites that offer this solution are Linkedin and Wordpress.

It is also strongly encouraged that organizations use strong encryption practices for personal information on company laptops and other portables devices like phones and USB. You should also consider using full disk encryption on systems that are not in use. Theft or loss of unencrypted data on electronic devices in one of the most common types of data breaches and strong encryption can negate it for the most part. In Chapter 4, we will discuss in more detail the different types of encryption options you have.

Encouraging affected customers the option of placing a *fraud alert* on their credit files can help to reduce the impact of a data breach and give customers reassurance that you are doing all that you can help protect them. A credit alert informs merchants that there may be fraud with this account and prompts them to request additional verification for that person's identity, often times this feature can be added free of charge.

References

https://ftc.gov/tips-advice/business-center/privacy-and-security/gramm-leach-bliley-act

https://cisecurity.org/controls/

https://hldataprotection.com/2016/03/articles/cybersecurity-data-breaches/
reasonable-security-becomes-reasonably-clear/

CIS Controls™. n.d. Retrieved from https://cisecurity.org/controls/

Gramm-Leach-Bliley Act. n.d. Retrieved from https://ftc.gov/tips-advice/
business-center/privacy-and-security/gramm-leach-bliley-act

Otto, P., and B. Kennedy. March 02, 2016. "'Reasonable Security' Becomes
Reasonably Clear to the California Attorney General." Retrieved from
https://hldataprotection.com/2016/03/articles/cybersecurity-data-breaches/
reasonable-security-becomes-reasonably-clear/

CHAPTER 5

Required Encryption Standards

This Chapter Will Discuss the Importance of Using a Certain Level of Encryption for any Information that You're Company Holds While It Is in Your Possession and When It Is in Transit (on Your Website, Sent to Third Party Partners, and so on) and How You Can Find Software that Will Do This for You

Encryption refers to the practice of converting information into a code in order to prevent unauthorized access to that information. Encryption is a huge part of protecting customer information and it will be one of the first thing's that investigator's check for if there is a security incident. The reason encryption is so important is because even if information is stolen from your company's possession if its properly encrypted then the information will have no meaning and be completely useless to the criminal. When it comes to lawsuits, if you can show that the information that was stolen from your company was not in plain text, but encrypted (ciphertext) it will significantly reduce or completely eliminate the money you would have to payout.

Firstly, I will explain some the different aspects of encryption that you need to aware of when coming up with an encryption policy. There are two states of data that you will come across while doing business, data at rest and data in transit. Data at rest refers to information that is stored by the company on company databases, on company computers and laptops, and so on. While data in transit refers to information while it is being sent to and from customers over the Internet, for example when a customer makes a payment online with their credit card on your website, it's your responsibility to ensure that their information is encrypted throughout the process. The second important aspect of encryption is the difference between hash functions and digital signatures. Hash functions refer to taking information and scrambling or changing it so that it is no longer readable by a person until it is changed back to its original form. A digital signature is when the algorithm can encode a document that is very difficult to duplicate. It the equivalent of a digital fingerprint ensures that when a person signs a document, such as a contract, that the signer is the only one associated with that document and records it. Digital signatures use a standard format called Public Key Infrastructure (PKI).

Types of Encryption

Individual file and folder encryption: This type of encryption only encrypts specific files or folders when the software is directly told to and is best when there are only a few files on a computer that need encryption.

Volume encryption: In this type, all files saved in a certain location will automatically be encrypted and is good for medium sized volumes of sensitive information.

Full disk or whole-disk encryption: This is when all file on a laptop or computer are encrypted, in this situation you will need to enter a password or provide an encryption key from a USB when powering on the computer in order to unlock your files.

Fortunately good encryption is built into modern windows and MAC OS X operating systems and it is available on some Linux system as well. On windows, you have Microsoft BitLocker a disk encryption tool included in Windows 7 and the Pro and enterprise versions of Windows 8.1 and Windows 10. In order to activate Microsoft BitLocker open file explorer and right click on your C drive and click on "Turn on Bitlocker." If you do not see this option then your version of windows doesn't support BitLocker. After enabling BitLocker you will be prompted to save a copy of the recovery key, this is very important because you will need this key in order to access your data. You can print it off, write it down or save it to a file whatever is most convenient for you. Apple Filevault is the built in encryption software for MAC OS X. To turn on Apple Filevault click on the apple symbol on the top left, go to system preferences then click on security and privacy and then filevault. Similar to BitLocker once you enable Apple Filevault you will be prompted to save a recovery key in your icloud account but you can also choose to write it down or take a picture, which I would recommend. In terms of third party encryption programs here are a few of the top ones on the market:

VeraCrypt: This software is free and is compatible with Windows, Mac OS X, and Linux. It is one of the most popular options and receives high ratings from both users and third party testers.

AxCrypt: is an encryption software with a free and premium version. It comes with a password manager and it has a feature that allows you to share encrypted data with others.

Gpg4win: This software provides military level security for encryption and to digitally sign files and e-mails.

Another alternative is to use your current anti-virus/anti malware solution, many such as symantec, Kaspersky and Sophos include encryption in their security suites or will offer it as a separate product. For side-by-side comparison of some of the best retail software you can visit this website Top 10 Reviews.

Another important aspect of encryption dealing with information that is in transit, this includes sending information via e-mail or carrying it around on a USB. It's important to note that once information is sent via e-mail or copied over onto a USB it is no longer protected by the encryption that is present on the machine that you copied it from. To protect data even in these situations company USB's should have their own encryption protection. You can use programs like Microsoft's

BitLocker To Go or purchase USB's that come with encryption software pre-installed such as IronKey, SanDisk and Kanguru. When it comes to **e-mail encryption** it's important to note that e-mail encryption can be inconvenient so you don't want to encrypt every e-mail that you send as a business, it would simply to be time consuming and unless the user is tech savvy there is a good chance they won't know how to decrypt it. However, in situations where you are sending highly sensitive information e-mail encryption is very important, otherwise anyone that is eavesdropping will be able to access the contents of your messages. Fortunately, most businesses won't need to worry about this as a legal liability. Since in most cases you are using another companies e-mail service unless there is some negligence on your companies part such as sending an e-mail to the wrong address you generally won't be liable if someone is able to access the e-mail in transit, that would fall on the e-mail provider. If you work for the government or another company that has sensitive information that you really wish not to get out, then here are some of your options for encrypting e-mails. Firstly, most e-mail suites such as gmail, outlook, and so on come with their own built in encryption options that you can use. I will be discussing how to configure this on three different platforms: Outlook, iOS, MAC OS X, Android, and Gmail as well discuss how to have a burner e-mail address (send e-mails anonymously).

Outlook: The first step to initiating encryption with outlook is to have a digital certificate. If your organization doesn't provide one, then you will have to create one. Follow these steps:

- Go to File > Options > Trust Center > Trust Center Settings > E-mail Security, Get a Digital ID.
- Choose which certification authority you want to receive a digital ID from
- You will receive the digital ID in an e-mail.

Now to set it up so that the digital signature can be attached to signed e-mails:

- Select Tools > Options and click the Security tab
- Input a name of your choice into the Security Settings Name field

- Make sure S/MIME is selected on the Secure Message Format box
- The Default Security Setting should be checked
- Under Certificates and Algorithms, go to the Signing Certificate section and click Choose
- In the Select Certificate box, choose your Secure E-mail Certificate if it hasn't been selected by default
- Check "Send these Certificates with Signed Messages"
- Click OK to save your settings and return to Outlook

To attach the digital signature:

- Click New Message
- Go to Tools > Customize and click the Commands tab
- In the Categories list, choose Standard
- In the Commands list, click Digitally Sign Message
- You can click and drag the listing onto your toolbar, so from now on just click that to add your digital signature
- To make it easy in the future, click and drag Encrypt Message Contents and Attachments onto the toolbar as well

Now at this point you are able to send someone an e-mail with you digital signature, which is a prerequisite for being able to send them an encrypted message that they can decrypt. You also will need them to send you an e-mail with their digital signature if you're going to be receiving encrypted from them, this is how outlook knows that it's coming from a trusted sender. Once you have each other's digital signatures saved in your address books, you can begin to exchange encrypted e-mails with one another using the Encrypt Message Contents and Attachments button we added earlier.

Encrypting E-mail Using Ios

Go into advanced settings and switch S/MIME on and change Encrypt from default to Yes. Now when you go to create an e-mail you should see a lock icon, click on it to close it and the e-mail will be encrypted. If the icon is blue then that means an encrypted e-mail can be spend to that person, if the icon is red that means that an encrypted e-mail can't be sent. This is usually because either they are out of your exchange environment (for example a different company) or you haven't installed their digital signature.

Similar to outlook a digital signature must be exchanged between recipients if you want to send encrypted messages:

- Go to the advanced settings menu and you will see an option to attach your digital signature to an e-mail.
- Once you receive the e-mail, Click the sender's address
- A red question mark icon will appear indicating the signature is untrusted. Tap View Certificate
- Tap install. When done, the install button will change colors to red and say "Remove." Click Done on the top right corner.
- Now when you compose a message to that person, the lock icon will be blue. Tap it to close the lock and encrypt your message.

OSX E-mail Encryption

To use OS X encryption with the default mail program, you first need to exchange digital signatures with the recipient. However, in order to make sure the encryption is effective you need to ensure that the person you are sending the information to is using a service that supports the type of encryption that you are using. For example in the case of gmail, in order for gmail encryption to be utilized, the receiver must be using a service that supports TLS encryption.

In order to make sure your company's information is properly encrypted, the first thing you're going to want to do is decide on which encryption algorithm you want to use. When it comes to digital signature generation, some acceptable algorithms are DSA, RSA, and EC. When it comes to hash functions your best bet is to use SHA-2 or SHA-3. Avoid using the following algorithms RC4, DES, Triple DES, SHA-1, and MD5. Regardless of the encryption solution that you choose, take some time to look at what type of encryption algorithms they are using, you want to ensure that they are running an acceptable algorithm or else despite the information being encrypted it may be so simple for an attacker to break that its essentially useless. You can usually find this information during the configuration process or you can look for the contact information for your vendor and inquire about what encryption algorithm they use.

Reference

https://toptenreviews.com/software/security/best-encryption-software/
?_ga=2.221999965.477177787.1526580777-1700569461.1504544859&
cmpid=ttr-bnd

—

CHAPTER 6

How to Offload Legal Liability onto Third Parties

This Chapter Will Discuss Third Party Solutions that You Can Use to Secure Your Data and Will Accept Liability if any Data Breaches Do Occur

In this chapter I will be discussing options for outsourcing the Cybersecurity portion of your business. For SMBs in particular outsourcing different portions of your Cybersecurity program is important to ensuring that your company is properly prepared. Many small business owners feel that their company is too small to be known and targeted by attackers but that is not the case. SMBs are one of the most preferred targets by hackers because they lack the staff and expertise of larger corporations. According to a study by Ponemon Institute's "2017 State of Cybersecurity in Small and Medium-Sized Businesses" report (see Chapter 6 appendix), 61 percent of SMBs had at least one cyberattack in the last 12 months. One of the best ways for a small business to make up for their lack of cybersecurity specific staff is to outsource it to a larger, specialized company. For larger corporations outsourcing still has many benefits that make it worthwhile. Firstly, I'll talk about the pros and cons of outsourcing (Sorokin and CDW (July 24, 2018). When Should You Outsource Cybersecurity?):

Benefits:

- Reducing Costs: Outsourcing all or part of your cybersecurity program can be far more cost effective than hiring full time workers or contractors, especially if you're unsure if you're going to have enough work for them to keep them busy eight hours a day. For example some service provider's charge as low as $75,000 a year for protection, where one average IT security specialist can cost you as much as 80,000 and that doesn't include the equipment you would have to purchase, benefits and other staff members.
- Allows you to focus on your core competency: By outsourcing cybersecurity your employees can focus all of their time and attention on innovating and creating more revenue streams for your business.
- Gives you more focused expertise: It can be difficult and time consuming to find employees with the expertise you need in cybersecurity. When you consider the amount of time it takes to train employees, it could be up to six months before a new hire is properly trained and working at a pace that makes him worth his salary. By outsourcing you can find specialists relatively quickly and for a low cost.
- It offloads liability in case of a cybersecurity incident: This is the most important benefit when it comes to information security law, in the event that the company you hire doesn't perform their job as promised you will not be liable for lawsuits from your affected clients.
- 24/7 client support: Most security provides provide 24/7 support 365 days a year, which is very important because security incidents can happen at any time and are impossible to predict.
- Gives you validation of your security posture: Using an external team to do a security assessment such as penetration testing, auditing or a vulnerability scan will give you an objective way of seeing how security your company truly is.

- Stay on top of rapidly evolving technology: Within every domain of cybersecurity there are new technology solutions being developed every year, for one organization it would be virtually impossible for you to stay current with all of these new tools across all of the cybersecurity domains. By using specialist security providers you can have access to the latest technology.

Cons:

- It requires trust in the company: Once you make the decision to outsource your cybersecurity, you are trusting this company to protect your sensitive information. You will lose control over how the data is handled and by whom, you need to make sure you have enough trust in the company you pick to handle it correctly.
- It's a supplement: Many security providers offer their services mainly as a supplement to your current security solutions and staff, it's not meant to be a complete replacement.
- Some staff will still be necessary: You will still need some security staff for the service provider to report to and coordinate with.

While the benefits for outsourcing can be huge, as with all legal processes you need to be very thorough when choosing a company. Here are a few things you want to consider when evaluating companies:

- References: Look up and ask the company you are considering hiring for references, read company reviews, search their rankings and don't just read up on them but call them if possible. Also run the company name on a few search engines and see what reviews you can find, past performance is a good indicator of future performance.
- Third-party certifications: Another indicator of a good MSSP are third-party certifications such as ISO 270001, which is an Information Security Standards. It's also a good idea to check

how long a potential service provider has been in business, a company that has been in business for 10 years is generally a safer bet than someone that has been in business for two years.

- Be aware of your compliance requirements and if they cover that: When looking to outsource you want to be certain of what laws you need to be compliant of. For example if you're a financial institution the cybersecurity standards you're legally obligated to meet will be different than a healthcare institution. You need to know what is required for your industry, in your area and discuss it with the company to make sure they can support you on that.
- Get it in writing: As with any legal agreement when you decide to hand over part of your business you want to make sure that you include it in your company contract that the third-party agrees to handle your data in the correct manner. If an incident occurs in the future you want to be able to prove that they were aware of your requirements and agreed to them.

When looking to outsource your IT security you want to look for Managed Security Service Provider (MSSP). These are vendors that charge an upfront fee along with an ongoing subscription to handle certain elements of security measures. Almost any element of IT can be purchased as a service, however some of the most common elements that you want to use MSSP for are:

- Audit Requirements
- Network Monitoring
- Patching
- Vulnerability Assessments
- Identity and Access Management
- Cloud Security
- Penetration Testing
- Web and E-mail Security
- Cyber Threat Intelligence

General Purpose (Robb n.d). 11 Top Managed Security Service Providers (MSSPs)

These MSSP are options for companies that need help with their general security posture, ensuring that they have all of the required security measures to both protect their assets and ensure that they meet their industries and countries regulator requirements. IBM is one of the best vendors when it comes to across the board services. It offers services in network protection, firewall management, vulnerability scanning, information event management, log management, IDPS, data protection, security intelligence analysis, web gateway management, unified threat management (UTM), secure software-defined wide area network (SD-WAN), adaptive security for hybrid cloud, endpoint security and Amazon GuardDuty services.

Symantec is another top vendor that offers a wide variety of services such as monitoring services, intrusion detection and prevention system (IDPS) management, hosted log retention, intelligence services and advanced threat protection, in addition to incident response and cyber skills development. Symantec performs the monitoring and management of the customers' security environment–everything from data collection to incident identification and interactive alerting, with dedicated security analysts to prepare and provide details and recommendations on incidents.

AT&T Threat Manager is a security event monitoring and management service. Threat correlation and analysis is performed via the AT&T Threat Intellect platform, which includes SIEM, big data and analytics. It is delivered as part of AT&T's Threat Management and Intelligence solutions. Device management is available for network security, data and application security, endpoint and mobile security. Service options include Internet and Intranet protection,

Mobile security, DDoS Defense, Firewalls, Web application protection, IDPS, e-mail gateway, endpoint security, encryption, device management, and token authentication.

References

https://keepersecurity.com/2017-State-Cybersecurity-Small-Medium-Businesses-SMB.html

https://biztechmagazine.com/article/2018/07/when-should-you-outsource-cybersecurity

https://esecurityplanet.com/products/top-managed-security-service-providers.html

"2017 State of Cybersecurity in Small & Medium-sized Businesses." n.d. Retrieved from https://keepersecurity.com/2017-State-Cybersecurity-Small-Medium-Businesses-SMB.html

Robb, D. n.d. "11 Top Managed Security Service Providers (MSSPs)." Retrieved from https://esecurityplanet.com/products/top-managed-security-service-providers.html

Sorokin, M.M., and CDW. July 24, 2018. "When Should You Outsource Cybersecurity?" Retrieved from https://biztechmagazine.com/article/2018/07/when-should-you-outsource-cybersecurity

CHAPTER 7

The Importance of Cybersecurity Specific Insurance

A Common Mistake Companies Make Is Assuming Their General Insurance Plan Will Cover Cybersecurity Incidents, Which It Often Won't. It's Important that Companies Have a Cybersecurity Specific Insurance Plan. This Chapter Will Discuss This and Give Some Options

In this chapter I will be looking at ways that a company can make sure they have coverage in the event of a data breach. The first important thing to note is that most general insurance plans will not cover you in the event of a Cybersecurity incident. Since, cybercrime is a fairly new liability for business, most insurance plans have not been revised to include it. You will most likely have to purchase it as a standalone service from an insurance provider. Cybersecurity insurance, referred to as cyber liability or data-breach liability insurance will provide you with coverage on things like data loss from data breaches, network outages, service interruptions and more depending on your provider. Unlike like other more general forms of insurance, cybersecurity insurance can vary significantly in price and coverage depending your provider.

What Are the Types of Coverage

Cybersecurity insurance comes in two forms, first party and third party.

First Party Cybersecurity Insurance

This is the type of coverage that you will need to file a claim if your business experiences a data breach. Any company that holds customer data can benefit from the protection of first-party cybersecurity insurance. For most non-IT firms, first part insurance will enough to cover you for the risks you will be facing. The benefits of first party insurance include getting compensated for:

- Notifying clients that there information was leaked
- Buying credit monitoring for customers affected by a breach
- Funding campaigns to restore your company's reputation after a data breach
- Compensation for income lost while you deal with the effects of the data breach
- Money for paying a ransom to the person who is holding your data hostage or threatening an attack (cyber extortionist)
- Money stolen through the crime

Third-Party Cyber Risk Insurance

Third party insurance covers businesses that are responsible for the systems that allowed the data breach to occur. This refers to tech companies and contractors that are responsible for ensuring the protection of the information such as cloud service providers, network administrators and cyber security personnel. If your company is responsible for handling the information of other companies this type of insurance is very important, if you're company only handles its own information then first-party cybersecurity insurance is probably all you need. The benefits of third party insurance include getting compensated for:

- The misuse, disclosure or theft of information that was on a system that you set up and were responsible for protecting.

- Failure to prevent the transmission of malware to a third party.
- Security breaches of employee confidentiality.

It's important to note that when a lawsuit is filed everyone that worked on the systems at fault will be considered liable for the breach in security. Therefore even if your business only worked a portion of the project, you could still face legal action if a security incident occurs, which is why it's important that if you do any work that involves another companies information that you have this type of insurance. This includes businesses and contractors/freelancers.

Things Cybersecurity Insurance Won't Cover

Cybersecurity insurance is a relatively new area and therefore they still don't cover all of the problem areas that companies face. Many insurance plans won't cover things like damaged reputations resulting in lower sales and theft of intellectual property such as product design and software code because it is hard to quantify. It's important to realize if you're company suffers a data breach and customers realize that there private information has been lost, you will lose some customers. Especially, if that information is used against them, for example they start to see weird purchases on their credit cards or people use the login information they got from your company to hack into their accounts on other websites. This loss of trust, will impact your clientele and eventually your revenue and you will have a hard time getting an insurance provider to cover your for that.

How to Select the Type of Cybersecurity Insurance My Business Needs?

The first thing to do is prepare a risk assessment and impact analysis. Here you need to review what your assets are, understand what the companies risks are and what the impact of a breach would be. You also need to identify the main vulnerabilities that exist in your current IT systems. Once you have a good idea of what assets you have and what risks exist for them, you should begin by seeking legal counsel. There are cybersecurity-insurance brokers, that have experience and expertise in picking cybersecurity policies that are tailored to specific businesses. You can use the brokers to get advice on choosing a plan that best suits your needs. Since cybersecurity insurance is still fairly new there are not a large amount of insurance providers to choose from, you usually have to go through major carriers such as AIG, Apogee Insurance Group, Chubb and Zurich. However, in the coming years as this industry continues to grow, you can expect more insurance providers to start selling stand alone cybersecurity insurance.

How to Reduce Premium Costs

Since premium costs are based on risk, cybersecurity insurance can be quite expensive because the perceived risk if high and it can lead to large payouts. Also, since they are often customized to fit each company's needs they can be even more costly. Other factors that will affect the price include the nature of the business and the type of data it stores, size of the company, number of customers and how you collect and store your data. However, there are ways that your company can reduce the costs. One is by implementing security policies and practices for your company. By implementing best cybersecurity practices for your industry you reduce the risk of your company suffering from a data breach and this will reduce the cost of your insurance.

A study by UPS capital (an insurance company) found that 55 percent of small businesses reported at least one data breach during the year and cyber attacks would cost these businesses between US $84,000 and $148,000 (Products and Services|UPS Capital). Additionally, 60 percent of small businesses that suffered a cyberattack would be out of business within six months. A major reason most of these companies go out of business is because they are unable to recover from the financial and reputational losses associated with these data breaches, have a contingency plan that features a solid cybersecurity insurance plan will significantly improve the chances of your business being able to bounce back from an event such as this. If you are feeling overwhelmed about your options for insurance and want to make sure you are fully covered a website called techinsurance.com lets you talk to an insurance agent for free and gets quotes for your business. In addition to implementing good security practices and policies for your company having a quality cybersecurity insurance plan is a great contingency plan to make sure that your business doesn't suffer in the event that a data breach occurs.

References

https://upscapital.com/product-services/cyber-liability-insurance/

Products and Services | UPS Capital. n.d. Retrieved from https://upscapital.com/product-services/cyber-liability-insurance/

CHAPTER 8

What Type of People and Policies Should You Have to Ensure You Are Complying with Regulations

This Chapter Will Talk About the Type of Experience You Want to Look for When Hiring an Employee into Your Cybersecurity Department to Ensure that They Will Be Mindful of the Legal Implications Your Company Will Be Facing

This chapter will apply to businesses that are looking to have their own internal legal teams to make sure that your business is compliant with all legal requirements. Firstly, I'll talk some policy practices to help ensure that your company will operate under their intended guidelines.

Establish an Information Security Policy (ISP)

An Information Security Policy (ISP) is a set of rules outlined by an organization to ensure that all the employees, contracts and third-party entities that work with your companies information will be expected to abide by. The purpose of creating this outline is to create a companywide approach to information security and ensure that all of your workers act in a way that will protect your companies information and make sure that your company is not breaking any laws.

Identify Your Companies Data and Systems

Your ISP should address all of the data, systems, facilities and users of information in your company identifying all of these identities is first step in creating an ISP. You need to know what information your company collects, where it is stored and who is handling that information within your organization. Start this by classifying you data because not all company information needs to be handled with as much care. By classifying your data, it helps you ensure that all of the information you have in your company has the appropriate type of security measures in place. There are typically four classifications of data within a company:

Public Information: This information can be distributed freely and doesn't need much policy around its handling and use. It's information can be freely distributed with no adverse effects because it is produced for public consumption. For example news releases and job announcements.

Business use only Information: This is information that is used in business processes and is unauthorized disclosure, modification or destruction is not expected to cause any serious problems for the organization, customers or partners. Some examples of this is internal policy manuals or company phone lists. For this level of information you will want to have moderate guidelines and policy in place but most of the Cybersecurity Legislations will not regulate this type of information.

Confidential Information: This is information that is used in sensitive business processes and its unauthorized disclosure, modification or destruction will have adverse effects to the company, its customers and/or its business partners. This includes information such as personally identifiable information, payment card information, protected health data, and bank account information. For this type of information and further you want to make sure you have very detailed policies regulating how this information is handled throughout your company. The information found in this category has significant regulation around it and those requirements need to be outlined and use in the creation of your company's security policies.

Restricted/Secret Information: This classification is the highest level of confidentiality and refers to extremely sensitive information used in business processes and its disclosure, modification or destruction will have serious consequences for the organization, its customers or its business partners. Some examples of this type of information would be medical records relating to mental health or sexually transmitted diseases and organizational information such as documents about mergers and strategic plans. Is this type of information is leaked there is going to huge financial and legal implications.

Once you have identified what type of information you are caring, the next step will be to ensure that all information is being handled with security measurements appropriate to their risk level. There are two main components to this, firstly you want to make sure you are aware of the legal requirements your company needs to do to be compliant. Secondly, you want to make sure that you have security measures in place that will protect the information from people who will try to steal it. As previously mentioned there is an interesting statistic found by UPS capital that found that 55 percent of small businesses reported at least one data breach per year and 60 percent of those small businesses would be out of business within six months. You want to do your best to ensure that information of the confidential or restricted level have strict policies on how they are to handled by workers within your organization. Most users do not know or frankly care that much about cybersecurity, about 50 percent of cybersecurity incidents can be attributed to user error. One of the most important ways to prevent this is to have strict rules on confidentiality, this means making rules that dictate exactly who in an organization is authorized to view, edit and destroy certain types of information. One of the best ways to prevent data leakages are to ensure that the information is known to as few people as possible and is stored on as few systems as possible. Information should only be accessible to people who only need it for their job functions and no one else, there should also be penalties in place for someone who shares information that is confidential to someone who is not suppose to have access to it. For those who do have access to information they should not have full discretion for what or how they use the information. There need to be parameters put on how information is to be used in this company so that everyone knows what is expected of them and how to do their daily processes in a secure way. Once you have established documentation on how each of the major processes of your business should be carried out, it makes it much easier to evaluate the processes to see how secure and effective they are and make improvements. With new regulations being introduced on a regular basis it's important to be able to not only make changes to your business processes but also be able to prove that you had the right security measures in place in the event that there is a breach and you are being audited by an external body. This framework will be utilized by:

- Internal auditors
- External auditors
- Third parties
- Employees

When creating an ISP you need to make sure that the policy is put into very simple and concise language to ensure that it is understood by everyone. Avoid ambiguous terms that could to misinterpretations and be sure that you know the exact meaning of the words you are using. For example I would suggest using terms like "must" or "need" rather than using terms like "should" or "its recommended," if something is to be done make sure that is plainly stated in the policies.

However, usually all the rules don't apply to all members of staff equally. In most ISPs more authority and flexibility are given to management and senior management to use their discretion in deciding who they share data with within the company. This is rightfully so because often times business situations are dynamic and you need to be able to act accordingly, but you should also capture this in your ISP. You can put in the policy what rules can be overruled by certain levels of positions, but generally you want to sure that your lower level employees have very strict guidelines and those guidelines should become more flexible as you go up the company hierarchy.

Perhaps the most important step in creating good ISP is to share it throughout your organization. You want to be careful how you do this because just making your employees read and sign a document doesn't necessarily mean that they understand its content and that they are ready and willing to abide by it on a daily basis. Therefore, in addition to simply having them read and sign it, one good alternative is to have a training session where you discuss the policy with new hires. You can take this opportunity to talk about the most important elements of the policy such as levels of confidentiality, data sensitivity, how to collect/use/delete data, maintain data quality, records management, confidentiality, privacy, appropriate utilization of IT systems, correct usage social networking, and so on. Another approach companies use is to have online modules that teach employees about their ISP and then tests them on the concepts at the end, using real world scenarios where they have to apply what they learned in a situation similar to what they will experience on the job. They will not be able to complete the module until they get a certain score, usually about 80 percent. This ensures that employees are not only familiar with the concepts in your ISP but they can also apply them in a practical way. Upon completion of the modules an e-mail would be sent to HR for their records so that they know that this employee has completed his onboarding training. Even if the online method isn't an option, I would suggest some sort of small test be given to new hires to ensure that they have properly understood your companies ISP policy, especially for positions that will be doing a large amount of handling sensitive data. Your ISP policy should also be stored on your network to be accessible to your employees at any time throughout their employment.

The next important aspect to discuss is how to build the right team to ensure that your company is protected in the event of data breach. Firstly, if are running a small business and your company isn't incorporated I would highly recommend considering incorporating it. This will ensure in the event that a data breach occurs and one of your customers is negatively affected that they cannot sue your personally. An incorporated company is considered its own separate legal person and this is good because that means the company will be held liable in the event of an incident and your own personal assets won't be at risk if your company is sued, if you chose to incorporate it. Aside from that, when you are looking to hire people you want to have an Information Security Lawyer either on staff or one that you can call in the event of an emergency. It's important that you have legal counsel that is specialized in dealing with cases regarding technology, which can be very difficult to find because many of the devices that we use right now are fairly new and traditional law degrees do not teach what is required for dealing with laws relating to cybersecurity. For instance say you company is accused of being negligent in its security defenses that resulted in ransomware infecting your company and eventually deleting some important customer medical information. In order for your lawyer to properly defend you they need to have a proper understanding of how ransomware works, how it infected your systems, what industry standards for defense are and more. You don't want a lawyer that only has expertise in law and would have to learn these things on the fly to defend you, you want someone with some technical background because they will be able to properly demonstrate your companies innocence to both technical and non-technical jury members.

Make Backing Up Data a Regular Function

In the event that your company is hit with a malware that encrypts or destroy company data, you will want to ensure that you have up to date backup of your information available to keep your business running smoothly. How often you backup your information depends on how valuable those particular files are. Records that are essential to your business should be backed up at least once per day, files that are moderately important or less should be backed up one per week or biweekly at the least. These backups can be keep on the network for easy access but it's more secure to keep a copy on an offsite location so that there's not a single point of failure in the event of an incident. Whether you do you backups manually or automatically its best to create a backup schedule so that you don't forget or miss a backup at a critical time. Some general tips for creating a backup routine are:

1. Backup your most important files at least once a day, sometimes even more depending on how critical it is to your business.

2. Keep a copy of a backup in a secure location, for example save it to the cloud, a fireproof safe or an offsite storage location.

3. Use software to facilitate your backup schedule. Many online backup services offer scheduled backups that can save individual files as you choose, automatically save files that have changed since the last backup or do your entire system on whatever schedule you pick.

4. Ensure you have a disaster recovery plan, this a documented plan that outlines how to get your business up in running in case of a **total** loss of your servers. This is might in case of things like earthquakes, tornadoes, hurricanes, snow storms, and so on.

5. Full test your backups: Many companies enact backup plans but many times those backups don't work, and they are unable to recover their data when they need it the most. Make sure to schedule full testing of your backups at least once every quarter to ensure that your backups work and you're able to recover your information in the event of an incident.

Provide Training for Your Employees

Ninety percent of all cyber attacks are executed with information stolen from employees who unwittingly give away their access credentials to hackers. Hackers often use a method called spear phishing where they send out fake e-mails, text messages or phone calls to trick employees into giving up sensitive information that they can use to gain unauthorized access or to get them to unknowingly download malware onto company systems. If it found that a data breach occurred because of employee negligence, you or your employee could be found liable for any of the damages that occur to customers as a result of that. Furthermore, if you never trained your employee on how to identify this phishing campaigns, then it becomes even more likely that your company will be found to be responsible for the data breach and all the damages that follow as a result of that. Therefore, it's important to train any employees that are going to be collecting or handling data on the proper procedures to follow to reduce the risk of a security incident, as well as giving them training on how to identify fake e-mails, texts, and phone calls.

Collecting and Handling Data

When training your employees some of the important things you want to highlight are:

- What information should be collected and which shouldn't: Only information that is absolutely necessary for business processes should be collected and depending on the process for which it should be collected, employees should be told exactly what information should be taken. There should also be instructions on how a business process should be conducted from start to finish and how the information collect is to be used throughout that process, that way if there is any deviation it can be quickly identified and corrected and it will be seen as an error the employee rather than on behalf of the business.

- How the information is to be secured should be outlined: Confidential information on paper should be securely locked away and only accessible by authorized personnel. All information on USB's should be encrypted so that in the event that they are losted, they will be useless to any unauthorized person that find them. You should have secure trash bins in your office spaces so that when you are ready to dispose of sensitive documents they can be shredded and placed in a secure bin so that they can't be removed and pieced together by someone else.

One good way to give employees training is through the use of online training modules. This is a very common training method in financial institutions, where all new employees are given online training modules that they must complete before they can begin working on regular business processes. The modules gives the employee's material to study and then tests them with both standard Q&A as well as live simulations of situations to see how they would respond. Employees are usually to get at least an 80 percent before completing the module and once they have been completed they will receive an online certificate that proves that they have completed the training. This will help reinforce their understanding of how to collect and handle person information and recognize phishing e-mails that will greatly reduce the risk of them clicking on an illegitimate e-mail or attachment. In addition to initial training upon being hired, employees should undergo continuous and regular training sessions to learn how to prevent new methods of cyber attacks.

Create an Internal Audit Team

An audit team is an internal group of experts responsible for helping your business manage Cybersecurity Threats through preventative programs as well ensuring compliance with all the legal standards that apply to your business. Your legal attorneys will work with both your audit department and your companies board of directors/management to address your potential cybersecurity risks. There are four key elements to developing a strong internal audit team:

Acquire Talent

You want to ensure that your audit team has the correct skillset, an important part of this is looking for people with experience specific to what your company is doing. You want to look for people that have worked in your industry, with a similar type of product/service and is knowledgeable about the legal landscape of your geographical location. Finding this type of specialized talent can be very difficult, a good alternative is to provide training and development for members of your audit team. It is not unusual for a company to invest well in security personnel and it can save you a lot of problems in the long run to ensure that your company is fully compliant with the law.

Make sure to audit the operational side of your business not just the technical. Usually companies focus solely on auditing the technical aspects of the company such as its firewall rules, app security, network security, and so on. However, it's important that all aspects of the company be evaluated equally, such as the operations processes of the company, how it interacts with its customers and vendors and in this context how the information the company collects is collected, utilized and protected is the most important aspect. For example one process that I often find gets overlooked are companies hiring processes. I'll often see on job postings, companies will say things such as "looking for a programmer with strong skills in Java" or "looking for someone with experience with Windows 10 OS." At face value it might seem like nothing is wrong, but making such specific statements on a job posting that will be accessible to the public can pose a security risk. By specifying exactly which software your company is running, you are making the life of any potential hacker much easier by giving them information on what they can exploit within your company. Before a company is breached, cybercriminals do what is called "reconnaissance," where they try to gain as much information about the company's network as possible so that they know what type of vulnerabilities the company has and how they can exploit them. By making the job ad to specific you can be unknowingly giving away sensitive information that can be used against you later on. This is an example of one the operational processes that audit would need to review to ensure that the business is more secure.

Keep Your Audit Team Connected with Other Cybersecurity Departments

It's important to ensure that your cybersecurity departments act as one coordinated program rather than several separate departments and the audit department is no exception. Your company's management should facilitate opportunities for the audit team to interact with key people in other departments. One approach some companies used is to implement a rotation of internal audit staff into and out of different cybersecurity departments, this way they increase their understand of each of the areas that they are supposed to regulate as well as become more aware of the other departments processes.

Use External Auditing

Relying strictly on internal auditing can have its own disadvantages, many times people can become biased if they have already audited a system or helped design a system. They tend to become reluctant to finding flaws in their work and are more likely to miss an error within that system. By opening up your company to external auditors that are neutral and often more critical of your business than internal employees you are more likely to get more suggestions on how your company can become more secure. Secondly, utilizing external audits gives to access to expertise you may not have within your company at the time. There are companies that specialize in auditing and using their services can give you cost effective access to industry experts. Lastly, one important aspect of auditing that is overlooked is performing audits on service providers and third parties. Third parties can be a huge weakness in your security program because they may not have the same level of cybersecurity awareness or preparedness as your company, making them a potential cybersecurity risks. By doing unannounced audits you can find potential weak points in your system, ideally the relationship should go both ways, you should periodically be performing cybersecurity audits of your third parties while allowing third parties to periodically conduct assessments of your company's information security.

References

https://globalnews.ca/news/2537715/can-law-enforcement-legally-access-data-on-your-smartphone-in-canada/

https://transparency.twitter.com

Bogart, N. February 25, 2016. "Can Law Enforcement Legally Access Data on your Smartphone in Canada?" Retrieved from https://globalnews.ca/news/2537715/can-law-enforcement-legally-access-data-on-your-smartphone-in-canada/

CHAPTER 9

Interacting with Law Enforcement

What Rights Do Government Officials Have When It Comes to Accessing a Companies Data on Clients/ Customers? When Do You Have the Right to Say No to an Investigator?

With the growing reliance on electronic devices such as smartphones and laptops, they now play a major part in criminal investigations. In 2016 there was a huge debate over whether Apple should comply with a US court order to hack into one of their iPhone's to help with the investigation of the San Bernardino Shooters. On one hand it could be viewed as a violation of people's privacy to release data that the company has agreed to keep confidential, between the customer and the company holding the data. However, businesses are also legally obligated to obey with court orders, so it can be quite a grey area and a difficult decision to make.

Legal Situations in Canada

In June of 2014 the Supreme Court of Canada ruled "police need a search warrant to get information from Internet service providers (ISPs) about their subscribers' identities when they are under investigation." According to this ruling a warrant is required by law enforcement except for the following circumstances:

1. If there is a reasonable law authorizing access.
2. If there are urgent circumstances, where the information required may prevent immediate bodily harm.
3. If the information being sought does not raise a reasonable expectation of privacy.

In a separate ruling in December 2014, the Supreme Court of Canada then said that police may conduct a limited search of suspect's cellphone without a warrant, but they must follow certain rules and the search must be directly related to the circumstances of a person's arrest and the police officers must keep a detailed record of the search. The rules are as follows: Bogart (2016).

1. The arrest must be lawful—This is the case for any situation; it just means if the arrest isn't lawful, then neither is the search.
2. The search must be incidental to the arrest and police need an "objectively reasonable" reason to conduct the search. These include: protecting police/the accused/the public; preserving evidence; discovering evidence such as finding more suspects.
3. The nature and extent of the search are tailored to the purpose of the search. This means police activity on the phone must be directly linked to the purpose they give.
4. Police must take detailed notes of what they looked at on the device as well as how it was searched (for example, which applications or programs they looked at, the extent of search, the time of search, its purpose and duration).

For law enforcement officials to proceed without a warrant they would need one of three purposes: protecting police or the public, preserving evidence or discovering evidence. According to this ruling, whether or not the phone is password-protected is not a determining factor, a suspect is within their right to remain silent and not unlock their phone, however police are also within their rights to confiscate the phone and attempt to unlock it. Furthermore, in a statement to Global News a spokesperson for the Department of Justice Canada made a comment on some of the rights of a police officers during investigations

The Criminal Code provides a wide range of judicially authorized powers that police can use to carry out investigations. These powers range from wiretap authorizations, which allow the interception of private communications, to search warrants, which allow the search of property including computers and smartphones and general production orders, which compel the production of personal information by third parties.

However, according to the statement before police can resort to these tools they must convince a judge that there are reasonable grounds to believe an offence has been or will be committed and that these actions will produce evidence. The representative went on to say:

"Further, a wiretap authorization, a search warrant and a general warrant can also be accompanied by an assistance order issued by a court, which compels a third party to provide assistance where that assistance may reasonably be considered as required to give effect to the authorization or warrant." "However, there is no specific power in the Criminal Code to compel a third party to decrypt or develop decryption tools, nor is there any requirement for telecommunications services to provide these services."

Legal Situations in the United States

The fourth Amendment of the U.S Constitution protects its citizens from unreasonable government searches and seizures and this protection extends to information held on computers and other electronic devices. The fourth Amendment applies across the entire country and in some states they have additional state laws that put further requirements on law enforcement that they must fulfill before have the right to an individual's *information*. In order for law enforcement to require access to customer information or to perform functions of an investigation such as wiretaps they will need a legal court order to do so. However, it's important to note that depending on where the data is stored affects whether or not the court order has jurisdiction. For example in a court case between Microsoft and the U.S government, Microsoft refused to comply with a warrant for e-mails on a drug trafficking suspect because the servers with the information where stored in Dublin, the capital of Ireland and therefore they would need an Irish court order in order to legally access the information.

The California Electronic Communications Privacy Act

This law prohibits any state law enforcement agency from taking user data from a company without first obtaining a warrant from a judge. This includes private user data such as e-mails, digital documents like word and pdf documents, text messages and location information stored on electronic devices. In the past law enforcement agencies could request user data from tech companies without having a warrant and naturally people would feel pressured into complaining out of fear of getting into trouble with law enforcement. This may seem like a foreign concept, something that wouldn't happen very often but according to the authors of this bill state Sens. Mark Leno and Joel Anderson AT&T received over 64,000 requests for location information in 2014, Verizon received over 15,000 requests for location data in the first half of 2014 with only a third coming with a warrant. In twitter's transparency (https:// transparency.twitter.com) report they stated that they received 4,363 government data requests in the first half of 2015 and complied 80 percent of the time. With the increase in digital communication since 2015 and all indicators suggest it will only increase, it's important to know that you are legally obligated not to give out information on California residents without a warrant. The exceptions to this rule is if the owner of a device gives a government entity permission to access his data or if a government entity believes a device has been lost or stolen they can access it in an attempt to identify the owner and return it to them. There is also an emergency provision, if a government entity believes that "an emergency involving danger of death or serious physical injury to any person requires access to the electronic device information" then they can access the information without having a government warrant. However, the agency will be required to file for a warrant within three days of obtaining data. There are similar data privacy protections in Maine and Utah.

Chapter 9—How to Automate Cybersecurity Compliance

This chapter will discuss options for making your companies IT compliance more efficient. There are two main areas of compliance that companies needs to worry about. The first is internal compliance, this refers to making sure that the procedures outlined by management is followed all of the employees within the company. Many times employees may not understand why management mandates that things be down a certain way and are tempted to not adhere to the rules for convenience or some other perceived benefit. One unfortunately common example is that many people still use company computers to visit pornographic websites, which not only is time wasting from a management perspective but searching untrusted websites like this also opens up the company to being exposed to potentially dangerous malware and is a security risk. From a legal point of view this type of compliance is less important because even though it is serious someone does break the rules and opens you up to a security risk, your company is typically not going to suffer a lawsuit as a result of this because it is an internal rule governed and enforced by your company itself. The more serious of the two is external compliance, which refers to adhering to rules laid out for your company by an external regulatory entity such as the government. External compliance can be quite tricky for a couple of reasons. Firstly, companies are not always fully aware of the rules within the industry or location and it's very difficult for you to ensure you are in compliance if you are not aware of what is required on your part. There are new laws being put in place almost every year regarding data privacy and staying on top of that it is a very difficult task. This is the first reason you should look into of using an automated tool to help your IT team stay ahead of what is required by your company. Secondly, external requirements can demand significantly more work by your company. Government rules can require things such as e-mail retention, installation of supervisory controls, hidden back doors for law enforcement, mandatory data breach notifications to all customers and more. Staying on top of the different laws is difficult enough for many companies that are more focused on developing their product and acquiring customers but you also need to know what each of these laws requires of you on a practical level to ensure that you are compliant. Unfortunately many cybersecurity laws tend to use somewhat vague language that makes it difficult for you to pinpoint exactly what needs to be done. Some of laws I mentioned earlier used to terms such as "reasonable" information security practices, which is not very specific. You want a solution that can help you clearly identify what is required from your end. Lastly, you want a service provider that can help you determine what the financial implications of non-compliance would be. At the end of the day the main purpose of being compliant to external entities is usually more about avoiding lawsuits and fees than just compliant for compliance sake. Therefore, getting a solution that can you help you do a cost ben-efit analysis of the potential dangers of being found in non-compliance with an external compliance is invaluable in ensuring that your business is as profitable as possible. Before I talk about potential solutions to IT compliance I want to highlight some of the most difficult areas for IT compliance and what makes them so difficult. As I discuss potential solutions I will look at how this solution could help you manage these areas of your IT infrastructure:

- Bring your own devices (BYOD)—This refers to personal mobile devices like smartphones and tablets, because these devices are not owned and configured by your company itself they bring along with them unique security vulnerabilities. Even though they are not owned by your company, if one of your company's employees bring a device into your environ-ment that doesn't comply with external security requirements and a data breach occurs, you will still be considered liable for that security incident. (Google Mobile Device Management, (Schiff 2018).
- Patch Management—Another important area of compliance is patch management, which can be a huge source of security vulnerabilities. Rami Sass, co-founder of WhiteSource Software stated that "In 2017, the number of third-party vulnerabilities discovered in commercial and open source software more than doubled, requiring CIOs to ensure that

their software was patched in order not to expose their organization to unnecessary risks," says Rami Sass, co-founder and CEO of WhiteSource Software, an open source security and license compliance management platform. Some common examples of the problems that can be caused by poor patch management are the Meltdown and Spectre vulnerabilities found in late 2017 or the Equifax breach that was caused because of the exploitation of a vulnerability in their web app. The vulnerability and the patch was published in march of 2017 but they failed to do the patch and were breached shortly after that in an incident that affected approximately 147.9 million U.S customers Sweet (2018). Equifax finds additional 2.4 million in U.S. impacted by 2017 data breach. Due to the amount of people affected and sensitive of the information, which was mostly social security numbers it is considered the largest leak of personal information in history.

- GDPR—This stands for the General Data Protection Regulation which went into effect on May 25th 2018. It affects all companies that collect or process data about Europeans, goods or services in Europe or receive, store or process EU personal data for corporate customers. Attorney Daniel L. Farris, the chair of the technology group at the law firm Fox Rothschild LLP had this to say "It is pervasive, impacting the entire enterprise, and [will require] active management/oversight of third party vendors." "Companies that collect or process data about Europeans, offer goods or services in Europe, or even receive, store or process EU personal data for corporate customers will likely have to comply. [And] compliance means … enterprise-wide data mapping and a data inventory, generally only using personal data as permitted by individuals after consent/opt-in, managing vendors, regularly auditing or assessing privacy compliance programs and respecting an individual's 'right to be forgotten,'" he explains. "Non-compliance can cost a company up to 4 percent of global turnover [gross revenue]." To help with GDPR he suggests "begin documenting data processing and resulting risk, including any applicable rights of the data subject, if you have not already," says Hawke. "GDPR Article 30 requires that every organization subject to the regulation must maintain a record of data processing activities." However, there are free tools, such as this template provided by Everlaw, that can help guide organizations. Hawke (2018). Open-Sourcing our GDPR Compliance Preparation for Articles 30, 32, and 35.

- Vendor Management—Similar to the difficulties with BYOD, getting third party vendors to comply with all of the regulations affecting your company is a difficult problem for IT personnel. If you outsource your data processing to any third party vendors, it is considered your responsibility just as much as theirs to ensure that they are handling your customer's information in a way that is in compliance with all of your regulatory requirements.

- Internet of Things (IoT)—The Internet of things refers to increasing number of devices that are connected to one another via the Internet. All of these devices are endpoints that can be used as a point of attack by a cybercriminal. Due to the large number of devices combined with how quickly new items can be added to a company's IoT architecture, it makes it very difficult for a company to ensure that all of these devices are adhering to the rules that they need them to follow.

- Lack of Subject Matter Experts—Some companies don't have the financial resources to spend on a department dedicated to IT compliance and hiring Subject Matter Experts can be very costly. Higgins (2018).

Now that we have outlined some of the most serious issues when it comes to security compliance, let's talk about some potential automated solutions that will save your IT staff time and make them far more efficient than manual processes. (20 Best Mobile Device Management Software in 2018 n.d.) Firstly I'll discuss options for dealing with the problem of mobile devices.

Cisco Meraki

This solution offers management for mobile devices as well as Macs, PCs and the entire network from a centralized dashboard. It gives you the ability to enforce device security policies, deploy software and perform remote troubleshooting on thousands of devices. Like IBM MaaS360 it offers over-the-air (OTA) centralized management, which means no hardware installation required combined with diagnostics and monitoring of mobile devices. It's built in systems Manager monitors each device and displays metrics such as client hardware and software information and recent location. It is also offered through customer pricing.

Highlights

- Scalable endpoint configuration
- On-device content management
- Secure support for BYOD initiatives
- Automatic device classification
- Automatically apply network policies by device type
- Analyze network activity with automatic reporting

InTune Enterprise Mobility+Security: This is a microsoft product that is designed to allow you to securely manage iOS, Android, Windows, and macOS devices from a single unified solution. It combines Microsoft Azure security with identity management solutions with legacy admin functions. It gives you the option of creating your own mobile management strategy that fits your needs and apply those management controls across your network devices. The starting price for it is about US $5.80 per user per month.

Highlights

- Mobile device and app management
- Advanced Microsoft Office 365 data protection
- Integrated PC management
- Integrated on-premises management
- Identity and access management

- Information protection
- Identity-driven security

IBM MaaS360

This is IBM's mobile device management solution. It also allows you to management iOS, macOS, Android, and Windows devices through a centralized portal. It provides OTA device enrollment so you can manage devices without having to install any hardware. It supports IoT Devices that use APIs for management, allowing you to secure them and the gateways that collect data from them. MaaS360 is offered through custom pricing.

Highlights

- Powered by Watson engine
- Multi OS and platform security
- Supports IoT devices
- Supports ruggedized Android devices and apps
- Supports Windows 10 to Windows 7 legacy PCs
- Provides secure container to store corporate content

Patch Manager (Cloud Management Suite)—This suite allows you to automatically patch your desktops, laptops, servers and remote users with security patches and software updates for Microsoft, MacOS, Linux and third-party vendors such as Adobe, Java and Chrome, Virtual Machines and IoT Devices. It comes with 24/7 support, training options in person, online and webinars. It also comes with a free trial so you can try the full product without having to commit any money. Its key features include:

- Custom Patches
- Automatic Scans
- Multi-Patch Deployments
- Network Wide Management
- Remote Protection
- Scheduled Deployment

- Subscription Services
- Vulnerability Scanning

SysAid

Sys has been serving over 100k admins globally for more than 15 years. It allows you to manage all your IT support from one dashboard. It includes a ticket management tool, IT asset management with a self-service portal. Key Features include:

- Multi-Patch Deployments
- Automatic Scans
- Scheduled Deployment

Naverisk RMM and PSA

Naverisk is described as an all-in-one monitoring and patch management solution for managed service providers and IT service teams for device monitoring with a built in ticket system. Key Features include:

- Custom Patches
- Automatic Scans
- Multi-Patch Deployments
- Network Wide Management
- Remote Protection
- Scheduled Deployment
- Vulnerability Scanning

Automated Compliance Tools

These are tools that can automate the process of ensuring that all of your systems are compliant with your Internal IT regulations. For this i'll be using an example I'm familiar with called CyberSmart. Cybersmart is a software that automates compliance by via an app that is installed on all of your company systems. This app can check your computer to see if it has predetermined security measures installed and running on your computer. For example if you have an internal rule that all company computers must have an active firewall running on your computer, you can have a developers of Cybersmart create a rule that will automatically scan all of your computers to see if the firewall is active and you can check via the online portal which systems have it and which do not. Cybersmart comes automatically with a basic set of rules based on common Cybersecurity best practices and you can get new rules custom made as needed. Also, CyberSmart offers automated GDPR compliance, as mentioned GDPR is a new Cybersecurity law in the EU that governs data protection and privacy for all individuals with the European Union. If your company collects any information from individuals in the EU it will be affected by this bill. Cybersmart will not only automate the process of checking if your compliant but it will also allow you to apply for your GDPR certification, but it will only allow you to do so when you are guaranteed to qualify for the certificate. Cybersmart is just one option when it comes automated compliance but the point is that tools like this are out there and they can make the process of being compliant much easier. Rather than having a whole team dedicated to identifying technology requirements, checking all of your systems and then getting the certification manually. Tools such as this can take care of about 75 percent of the work and you only need staff to operate the tool, create the policies and make changes to the systems that are identified by the tool as being non-compliant. When looking for an automated compliance solution the features you want to look for are:

- Deployable Apps
- Integratable with your company Operating Systems
- Live Customer Support 24/7
- Policy Distribution Capabilities
- Willing to work with managed service providers if you don't manage you own IT systems

References

https://cio.com/article/2382445/compliance/compliance-7-biggest-it-compliance-headaches-and-how-cios-can-cure-them.html

https://thestar.com/business/economy/2018/03/01/equifax-finds-additional-24-million-in-us-impacted-by-2017-data-breach.html

https://blog.everlaw.com/2018/03/05/gdpr-compliance-preparation-articles-30-32-35/

https://financesonline.com/mobile-device-management/

https://blueprintsys.com/blog/the-top-6-reasons-compliance-demands-complicate-your-software-requirements/

Bogart, N. February 25, 2016. "Can Law Enforcement Legally Access Data on Your Smartphone in Canada?" Retrieved from https://globalnews.ca/news/2537715/can-law-enforcement-legally-access-data-on-your-smartphone-in-canada/

Hawke, L. March 02, 2018. "Open-Sourcing our GDPR Compliance Preparation For Articles 30, 32, and 35." Retrieved from https://blog.everlaw.com/2018/03/05/gdpr-compliance-preparation-articles-30-32-35/

Higgins, T. February 06, 2018. "6 Reasons Compliance Demands Complicate Requirements." Retrieved from https://blueprintsys.com/blog/the-top-6-reasons-compliance-demands-complicate-your-software-requirements/

Schiff, J.L. May 09, 2018. "5 Biggest IT Compliance Headaches and How to Address them." Retrieved from https://cio.com/article/2382445/compliance/compliance-7-biggest-it-compliance-headaches-and-how-cios-can-cure-them.html

Sweet, K. March 01, 2018. "Equifax Finds Additional 2.4 Million in U.S. Impacted by 2017 Data Breach." Retrieved from https://thestar.com/business/economy/2018/03/01/equifax-finds-additional-24-million-in-us-impacted-by-2017-data-breach.html

20 Best Mobile Device Management Software in 2018. n.d. Retrieved from https://financesonline.com/mobile-device-management/

CHAPTER 10

Recap and Conclusion

This Chapter Will Recap the Most Important Elements of the Previous Chapters and Highlight Key Takeaways for the Readers

With the increasing number of cybersecurity threats, there are more risks to data breaches then at any point in time. If you are a business that collects significant amounts of data from your customers it's very important that you meet your national, state/provincial and industry cybersecurity standards. In most places you will be required by law to provide adequate protection of your clients information or else you will be liable for any losses to privacy or financial losses that your customers suffer as a result of leaked information. In order to meet this standard you company will typically be expected to have the following in place:

1. **Physical Protection:** This includes things like making sure you have locks on your doors, security staff. All the necessary tools to secure the companies physical location and physical documentation. This is usually one of the more neglected areas of information security but many times in the workplace people will leave documents on their desk or in unlocked cabinets and that is a security risk. If someone has bad intent they can quickly take a picture of the document and all of your other security measures have been made meaningless.

2. **Organizational Measures:** This means having protocols on how employees should conduct themselves to reduce the likelihood of security incidents due to negligence. This includes have procedures on what information should be collected from customers, how

the information should be handled, who should have access to the employee information and making sure controls are put in place to enforce these boundaries. It's become commonplace in some industries such as financial institutions to implement mandatory information security training for their employees, through online modules course that they must complete. It's a cost effective way to provide training and once completed you know how proof that they were properly trained, so in the event of employee misconduct they can't claim that they didn't know what they were doing was wrong.

3. **Technology Measures:** In regards to this, your company should require that employee passwords have a certain level of complexity in order to prevent them from being easy for a hacker to brute force attack. Typically companies will require that the password be at least eight characters long with at least one lower and uppercase letter, a number and a special character. Your company computers should have an active anti-malware suite running on it and it should have an active encryption algorithm on it, if it contains highly sensitive information. This also includes encryption of information resting on company assets such as laptops, information that is contained on USB's and e-mails containing highly sensitive information.

All of these measures are meant to protect lawsuits by proving that you did your due diligence to protect your customers information, the three main types of lawsuits you need to be concerned about are as follows:

Employee Errors: This is a situation where an employee does something unintentionally that results in a breach of privacy of an individual.

Employee Misconduct: This is a situation where an employee intentionally accesses information that are not authorized to see. To be safe employees should only be given access to information that is essential for them to do their job and nothing more, in information security this is covered under the principle of "least privilege."

Data Breaches: This lawsuits covered situations where information is leaked due to malicious activity by an external party. In order to reduce the likelihood of being found liable for these breaches it's very important you meet industry standard with your security measures.

We discussed the importance of having a cyber security specific insurance as a failsafe in case your company does suffer from a data breach and suffers financial losses. Many traditional insurance plans will not cover cybersecurity costs, therefore it is important that you ensure that your service does or get one that will cover you.

Another contingency plan we discussed offloading the responsibility onto third parties. One way you can do this is through cloud solutions, by offloading the storage of your data into a cloud solution any data breaches that occur will no longer be a liability for you but for your service provider, provided security is one of the features they promised you. This is a good alternative if you are a small company and don't want to be burdened with implementing all these different cybersecurity measures.

Lastly, I looked at what type of people you should be looking to hire to ensure that you are fully compliant with information security law in your area. When hiring you need to make sure your acquire the right talent for your department. It should include people with knowledge of the industry, knowledge of the laws in your specific geographical area and the areas in which your company operates and collects data and lastly you need someone with the technical knowledge to understand how your company infrastructure works and what changes you need to make to be fully compliant.

About the Author

Shimon Brathwaite, Former coop student in Ryerson University's Business Technology Management program who specializes in Cyber Security. He works as a Freelance Writer on Information Technology for Bussinessnewsdaily.com, an author at ThreatTracer.ca and a published author with Business Expert Press with books on Information Security Law and Cyber Threat Intelligence. During his time at Ryerson University throughout his works terms he accumulated three years of experience in Information technology and worked in Cybersecurity in the Areas of Cyber Threat Intelligence and Access Management at CIBC, TD and Scotiabank. I began working at Scotiabank as a network analyst where I worked with the Systems Architecture team to provide network support to branches internationally. I coordinated active directory and server backup centralization for 13 countries across the Caribbean. I then worked as an Information Security Coordinator where I secured infrastructure resources by implementing sustainable access management practices and performed data analysis and created reports using excel that were used by C-level executives for identifying trends within the bank. As a Threat Intelligence Analyst for TD I was responsible for identifying the most interesting and potentially dangerous attacker activity on the Internet. Working with other security analysts to analyze recent security incidents and creating actionable Intelligence. Creating intelligence reports that will be distributed to IT teams throughout the bank and utilizing intelligence feeds to determine what changes need to be made to improve bank security. He then founded ThreatTracer a Cyber Threat Intelligence Company in Ryerson's Digital Media Zone, the number one ranked Business Incubator in Canada. ThreatTracer is a Cyber Threat Intelligence Service provider for small to medium sized businesses looking for a proactive Cybersecurity solution to improve their security posture. Its infeasible for a business to perfectly defend against all cyber threats with new malware being designed and weaponized everyday, Threat Intelligence is necessary to make sure businesses dedicate their limited resources to their most probable threats.

Index

OTHER TITLES IN OUR BUSINESS LAW AND CORPORATE RISK MANAGEMENT COLLECTION

John Wood, Econautics Sustainability Institute, Editor

- *Preventing Litigation: An Early Warning System to Get Big Value out of Big Data* by Nelson E. Brestoff and William H. Inmon
- *Understanding Consumer Bankruptcy: A Guide for Businesses, Managers, and Creditors* by Scott B. Kuperberg
- *The History of Economic Thought: A Concise Treatise for Business, Law, and Public Policy, Volume I: From the Ancients Through Keynes* by Robert Ashford and Stefan Padfield
- *Buyer Beware: The Hidden Cost of Labor in an International Merger and Acquisition* by Elvira Medici and Linda J. Spievack
- *The History of Economic Thought: A Concise Treatise for Business, Law, and Public Policy, Volume II: After Keynes, Through the Great Recession and Beyond* by Robert Ashford and Stefan Padfield
- *European Employment Law: A Brief Guide to the Essential Elements* by Claire-Michelle Smyth
- *Corporate Maturity and the "Authentic Company"* by David Jackman

Announcing the Business Expert Press Digital Library

Concise e-books business students need for classroom and research

This book can also be purchased in an e-book collection by your library as

- a one-time purchase,
- that is owned forever,
- allows for simultaneous readers,
- has no restrictions on printing, and
- can be downloaded as PDFs from within the library community.

Our digital library collections are a great solution to beat the rising cost of textbooks. E-books can be loaded into their course management systems or onto students' e-book readers.
The **Business Expert Press** digital libraries are very affordable, with no obligation to buy in future years. For more information, please visit **www.businessexpertpress.com/librarians**. To set up a trial in the United States, please email **sales@businessexpertpress.com**.

CPSIA information can be obtained
at www.ICGtesting.com
Printed in the USA
BVHW071344140920
588712BV00013B/1015